CW01497295

You know when someone is
they convey the deep experi
they are coming from a pla
concern for every child. We
book. It's beautifully written, very funny and it sounds as
though she's alongside you as you navigate the complex
world of education in general and being a SENDCO in particular. A fantastic resource.

The role of the SENDCO is not an easy one. In this book,
Being a SENDCO, Ginny Bootman acknowledges some of
the many challenges, reassures the reader that it's okay
not to know everything, and then provides a wealth of tips
to help ease the load. Highlighting the empathy-based
approach that is core to her work, Ginny outlines a range
of practical examples for developing positive relationships
to get the best from pupils, parents and colleagues. *Being
a SENDCO* is full of invaluable, easy-win ideas to help the
busy SEND leader save time and effort in their demanding
yet extremely rewarding role. It is a book of little gems!

A wonderful book that strikes the delicate balance of
being positive yet honest and realistic about the SENDCO
role. Reading it feels like going for a coffee, cake and a chat
with an experienced colleague. And not just any colleague
... one who can help you navigate everything from tricky
conversations with families and facilitating staff training
on SEND to finding bargain SEND resources from pound
shops!

There are numerous practitioner-written books that are heavy going, and when you reach the end you really have to think about whether what you've learned has been helpful. What I love about *Being a SENDCO* is that you can pick it up and find well-explained nuggets of advice on every page. The 113 tips are not obscured by the strait jacket of trying to show how academic the book is.

From the foreword, which demonstrates the complexity of the job, through to the last section on working with outside agencies, I'd recommend this book to those aspiring to be a SENDCO and the most experienced practitioners.

Reading the book is like sitting down with an experienced mentor for a series of conversations over a coffee (maybe a glass of wine!). The tips are pragmatic and achievable, and I will definitely be ordering a copy for our (new in post) SENDCO.

If this is the area you want to work in, then I unreservedly recommend *Being a SENDCO* for an honest insight into the job and plenty of useful advice.

VIC GODDARD, CO-PRINCIPAL, PASSMORES ACADEMY, CEO, PASSMORES CO-OPERATIVE LEARNING COMMUNITY

Ginny's experience, humour and candour are the perfect guiding hand for SENDCOs who are new or looking for new directions in a role that has grown in size and importance in recent years. This book is packed with down-to-earth, doable ideas delivered in bitesize chunks to support and scaffold you in your role of supporting and scaffolding the children and adults within your community. Well worth reading and enacting.

POOKY KNIGHTSMITH, KEYNOTE SPEAKER

What a great book! I am not a SENDCO but I found that reading this enabled me to develop the empathy that Ginny mentions so many times for those in that role. I really loved the layout of the book – 113 tips – as it enables the reader to dip in at any point. The tips are quick, easy reads and cover everything. This is a great book for those considering being a SENDCO and also for those in the role already. It is also a great book to have on the staffroom bookshelf so that others can read it and understand the multifaceted nature of the role and just what being a SENDCO entails.

TORIA BONO, PRIMARY TEACHER, AUTHOR OF *TINY VOICES TALK*, HOST OF 'TINY VOICE TALKS' PODCAST

Every school's SENDCO is the beating heart of its inclusive practice. It's a role which calls for compassion, tenacity, determination, alchemy, resourcefulness, kindness, botheredness, purposefulness, care. Every school should have a Ginny championing their SENDCO when the tensions of the job are taut and they're running on fumes. And now they can with this wonderful book! Square Peg loves Ginny's 113 tips which are drawn from a deep well of professional wisdom and experience, sharing how to embody and deliver hope, love and joy in every school and for every child struggling to fit. Ginny shares how grit can be nurtured into shining baroque-sized pearls of achievement through the relationships and improved outcomes for children, young people, their families, colleagues and wider communities. Highly recommended for all professionals in SEND education and leadership alike. This book is not just for SENDCOs – it's guaranteed to make anyone who reads it 10% braver every day.

ELLIE COSTELLO, THERAPEUTIC PARENT, CAMPAIGNER, AUTHOR, DIRECTOR, SQUARE PEG

Clearly, this book is about the most important people in education: the children and young people. Ginny Bootman has created an immersive space for us all to feel supported and guided in the most important of roles – that of a SENDCO. She helps us to understand the challenges and the frustrations met by young people, parents and teachers in the world of SEND, along with a fantastic set of tips, thought-provoking strategies and a space where we can all feel supported.

Her beautifully crafted book has empathy; empathy which is driven by the need to get the best available support and help for children and young people within a complex education system. The articles, references and thorough research which Ginny Bootman shares with us supports why there are so many issues within our education culture and system, and this is to be highly commended.

This is a book for any teacher, parent or educationalist alike. You will not be able to put it down. It's a personal journey as well as a professional reflection of what we need to do to ensure that every child in every school has their individual needs met to the best of our ability.

NINA JACKSON, AUTHOR, AWARD-WINNING SPEAKER, MENTAL HEALTH AMBASSADOR, EDUCATION CONSULTANT, SEND SPECIALIST, TEACH LEARN CREATE LTD

The role of SENDCO is arguably one of the most important in any school. Taking on the role can seem daunting and the list of responsibilities endless. What Ginny Bootman has done in this wonderful book is distil her wisdom into snack-sized chunks so that anyone who is in the role now has a definitive guide as to what to do in every conceivable situation. This is a must for any SENDCO's bookshelf!

JOHN TOMSETT, EDUCATIONAL CONSULTANT, ERSTWHILE HEAD TEACHER

INDEPENDENT
THINKING
ON ...

BEING A SENDCO

Ginny Bootman

113 TIPS FOR BUILDING RELATIONSHIPS,
SAVING TIME AND CHANGING LIVES

independent
thinking press

First published by

Independent Thinking Press
Crown Buildings, Bancyfelin, Carmarthen, Wales, SA33 5ND, UK
www.independentthinkingpress.com

and

Independent Thinking Press
PO Box 2223, Williston, VT 05495, USA
www.crownhousepublishing.com

Independent Thinking Press is an imprint of Crown House Publishing Ltd.

Edited by Ian Gilbert.

The Independent Thinking On ... series is typeset in Azote, Buckwheat TC Sans,
Cormorant Garamond and Montserrat.

The Independent Thinking On ... series cover style was designed by Tania Willis
www.taniawillis.com.

British Library Cataloguing-in-Publication Data
A catalogue entry for this book is available from the British Library.

Print ISBN 978-178135424-7
Mobi ISBN 978-178135425-4
ePub ISBN 978-178135426-1
ePDF ISBN 978-178135427-8

LCCN 2022951757

Printed and bound in the UK by
Gomer Press, Llandysul, Ceredigion

In memory of Pat Blacker

FOREWORD

A shoulder.

An ear.

A voice.

An advocate.

A champion.

A mouthpiece.

A showcase.

A brainstorm.

A calm in the storm.

A break in the clouds.

A light in the dark.

A family counsellor.

A family mediator.

An interpreter.

A chaperone.

A coach.

A fan.

A referee.

A messenger. (Don't shoot.)

A way through.

A way out.

A way in.

The one who listens.

The one who knows.

The one who cares.

A friend.

A critic.

A challenge.

A hard stare.

A look of love.

The educational professional who campaigns tirelessly on behalf of the children who need more support than most to navigate a system that, at times, seems purposefully set up to make them fail.

A rock.

A lighthouse.

A signpost.

A crossroads.

A bridge.

A map.

A guidebook.

An encyclopaedia.

A facilitator.

A fixer.

A breaker.

A ducker and diver.

A risk taker.

A forgiveness seeker, not a permission requester.

An iterator.

An inventor.

An innovator.

A renovator.

A restorer.

A curator.

A creator.

A pioneer.

A navigator.

A confronter.

A holder to account.

A holder of standards.

A holder of hands.

An 'If at first you don't succeed, try again'.

A 'won't take no for an answer'.

A 'things can only get better'.

A smile maker.

A promise maker.

A tea maker. (Coffee also available.)

The one who knows where the biscuits are kept.

The one who always has tissues.

The one who knows where the loos are.

A transcriber.

A photocopier.

A filing cabinet.

A contacts list.

A secretary.

A calendar sorter.

A meeting organiser.

A room arranger.

An ambiance creator.

A switcher-off of the lights and a locker-up at the end.

A shot in the arm.

A shot in the dark.

A shot at life.

A starter.

A finisher.

An everything in-betweener.

A reassuring face in a crowded room.

A smile on a bad day.

A smile on a good day.

A hug when you win.

A bigger hug when you lose.

A keeper of promises.

A keeper of secrets.

A keeper of the flame.

That first hope.

Our last hope.

An expert.

An ally.

A connection.

A relationship.

A traveller on other people's roads.

A wearer of other people's shoes.

A SENDCO.

IAN GILBERT

ACKNOWLEDGEMENTS

This book would not have been possible without the help and support of all of my cheerleaders – those amazing individuals who span my home and educational life and who support me and inspire me in everything I do.

Thank you to the amazing team at Independent Thinking Press. Their support, patience and kindness have been amazing, especially Ian Gilbert and Emma Tuck who have guided me through this fascinating experience.

Huge thanks go to my family: to Aunty P, my son George and husband Glenn who are there cheering in the background when it all gets a bit much.

Thank you to all the teachers, parents and children with whom I have had the pleasure of working. Every day you teach me something new.

The most important thank you goes to my amazing mum Pat Blacker, my chief cheerleader, who always encouraged me to be myself.

CONTENTS

CONTENTS

CONTENTS

FIRST THOUGHTS

It is hard being a SENDCO. I should know (and I have been a head too!).

It isn't just the job, which is as challenging as it is rewarding, on a good day. It is also about the little things.

Have you ever had a time when you felt overwhelmed and you retreated, snail-like, into your shell, hoping things would sort themselves out? And what about that spiky email you received this morning? How is that going down? And when that parent raised their voice at you? How did you feel?

Then there are those times when you started to question your knowledge and expertise right in the middle of an important meeting and ended up losing your confidence and saying nothing (and then kicking yourself afterwards).

I know you have been there because I have been there too. That is why I wanted to write this book – to share with you many practical ideas to help you be the best SENDCO you can be, the SENDCO your children need you to be, the one you know you can be.

Perhaps the biggest lesson of all – and I am going to put this out there, right from the start – is this one: you don't know everything, and that is okay.

There are too many issues, too many children, too many families, too many situations and too many variables. No one knows it all, so beware those who think they do. It isn't only okay to say you don't know, it is you at your professional best. It isn't a weakness but a strength. I know that now, but it took me a while to learn.

My teaching career began with my training in Liverpool. It was such a great place to get a real feel for what lay ahead. Tough schools with tough teachers. No time for empathy. It was all about survival. I remember beginning teaching practice and being faced with a teacher who was very much on the edge. She would teach with perspiration dripping down her forehead, clearly in a constant and draining state of high alert. A teaching assistant approached me and said, 'Our number one job is to stop her from having a breakdown.' We just about managed it.

Fast forward four happy and challenging years to my first proper teaching job in Gateshead. Another tough school with some amazing children and now my own class. At the end of my first year, a parent sent me the loveliest card thanking me for everything I had done for her son. He was a fabulously challenging Year 6 child. His mother said I had given him the time and understanding that no one else had ever given him. A seed was planted in my brain.

Fast forward five more years. I had moved to Northamptonshire and was working in a school in Kettering. A Year 2 mother came to see me one day to say that her son found it difficult to write on A4 paper due to his fine motor difficulties. I said, 'No problem. Let's make his worksheets A3 size to help him.' You would have thought I had given her the world. Another seed.

In 2005, I not only became a teaching head in a small village school in Northamptonshire but also the school's SENDCO. Those were the days! To be honest, the SENDCO role was very different back then. I had so much else to do with teaching and leadership that the SENDCO role was a small part of my job. Four years later, after having my son, I returned to being a class teacher and now, without the headship duties, I could really take a look at those SEND seeds that had been planted previously.

Even as a class teacher, I began to understand the power we have to make a difference for the children who need us most, often through little things. And those little things start with listening carefully and then responding with creativity, determination and, of course, empathy. And with those three magic words: I don't know.

Over my career, I had come to learn that by making myself a bit more vulnerable, by having the confidence to admit I didn't have all the answers, I was able to build bridges with everyone with whom I worked. The families you come across meet enough experts; they need a human being. They need you at your professional, honest and compassionate best.

This book is designed to help you be that best, combining your professionalism with empathy, the ability to listen properly and a desire to understand what the lives of others are like and how you can help. It is a book full of tips to save you time and energy, little hacks to help you overcome obstacles and bumps in the road, and proven strategies that will help you build more effective relationships.

These relationships will benefit everyone who comes into contact with the amazing children in our care. It also extends to parents (a word I am using to refer to all individuals who have guardianship and a duty of care of a child or children) and to the professional teams outside the school environment who play a part in helping children.

Together, we can help children, often against the odds and even when the system seems to be working against us.

And we can love our role too; I should know.

113 TIPS

1. THE IMPORTANCE OF HAVING A NETWORK AROUND YOU

You aren't alone. I know it feels like it at times, but you aren't. What are you doing to make sure you are building a great support network around you?

In recent years, I have been lucky enough to work alongside fabulous SENDCOs in a multi-academy trust (MAT). We became a great team. We all brought our own lived experiences to each meeting, which meant that between us we had a wonderful breadth of knowledge. We all acted as each other's sounding board too, something all SENDCOs need. A critical friend to bounce ideas off in a non-judgemental but honest way.

Despite our breadth of knowledge, we also knew we had gaps. Everyone does. Once we had identified them, we were then able to organise the appropriate training to fill those gaps. This coordinated group effort gave us a great sense of security.

You may be the only SENDCO in your school, but you still need a network, even if you have to cast your net a little further afield to find it. Post-COVID-19, I am now being asked to speak at SEND events and conferences across the country. Make sure you come along! The SEND community is such a welcoming group, and I know you will be able to ask for all the guidance and support you need, both on the day and then through the new connections you have made.

2. THE POWER OF SOCIAL MEDIA

A face-to-face network is great, but it is also important to tap into online networks. They are such an invaluable source of ideas and support.

I joined Twitter in 2019, and I have never looked back. It has provided me with so many amazing contacts and is the best continuing professional development (CPD) you could wish for with regard to SEND. There are many useful SEND networks on Facebook and Instagram. I would strongly suggest that you give the world of social media a go, even if it is something that terrifies (or bores) you.

I was sceptical about joining these online groups at first; however, I have been proven wrong. Through these platforms, I have made amazing contacts, I have learned a great deal, I have people on hand who can answer my questions, day or night, and I have found out about so many SEND events – online, in person and often free.

If you are concerned about any of your questions and conversations being in the public domain, you can get (and give) advice through direct messaging. You can also join closed groups where you can ask specific questions about SEND.

To start with, make sure you follow me on Twitter – @SendcoGirl. Say hi, and I will help you find your feet. You will love it, I guarantee.

3. READ A BOOK OR JOIN A WEBINAR

'Every day is a school day' is such a well-known saying in education, but it is one in which I firmly believe. While on social media, I look out to see if there are any webinars that I think would benefit me professionally or personally. I watch out for anyone who interests me, and I view their webinars (either live or at a later date, when you can pause or re-watch parts of particular interest). It is fascinating to me that the authors I enjoy reading are often amazing speakers too. I like it when I read a book and can hear the author's voice speaking to me in my head. Often, webinars are up to an hour long, but they also include question-and-answer sessions, so you are getting a truly personalised professional development session from an inspirational person.

I am one of those people who likes to write notes in the book I am reading about the parts that really appeal to me or that I might want to refer to in the future, while others prefer to read eBooks. Either way, I would highly advocate listening out for recommended books on SEND. I use social media such as Twitter for recommendations. I find that if I own my CPD, I am more likely to enjoy it and learn from it. Own your own CPD too! There are also lots of free podcasts out there featuring lots of interesting ideas on special needs by people who are doing the same job as us. In this area, there seems to be a true feeling of sharing rather than a hierarchy.

4. SEND AND THE EUREKA MOMENT: PART I

When did you first realise you had a passion for being a SENDCO? And when did you utter your first SEND-related 'eureka'? The moment when you grasped that this was the job you were put on this earth to do?

For me, it occurred thanks to one particular child. I had been a SENDCO for many happy years when, always willing to learn new things, I went on a course to help me understand the specific needs of a child in my care. That day changed forever how I approached my SENDCO role. I suddenly had a moment of utmost clarity and understood, perhaps for the first time, what was important in my role and in my work with children.

Anyone who has heard me speak or followed me on Twitter will understand what I mean when I say that I suddenly knew the road I needed to follow wasn't a yellow brick one but an empathy one. I have been skipping that road ever since.

The approach we explored on that day unlocked in me a greater understanding of how I, as a SENDCO, could help children to feel safe, secure and valued in a genuine and understanding way. It was the key to revealing my true potential as a SENDCO. And what was the course that so changed my approach to my work? It was one that considered the work of Dan Hughes and Kim Golding and their PACE approach, which demonstrates the many benefits of employing *playfulness*, *acceptance*, *curiosity* and, of course, *empathy* in all your interactions.[1]

---

1 See K. S. Golding and D. A. Hughes, *Creating Loving Attachments: Parenting with PACE to Nurture Confidence and Security in the Troubled Child* (London: Jessica Kingsley Publishers, 2012).

- **Empathy.** And lots of it. My #FollowTheEmpathyRoad approach is right at the heart of all my work on a daily basis. You will have noticed by now that it is running through this book, too, like 'Bridlington' in a stick of rock.

Easy really.

5. SEND AND THE EUREKA MOMENT: PART II

Learning about a new strategy is one thing. Translating it into school-based practice is another – the real test of whether a day spent on an out-of-school course is worthwhile. Armed with my new acronym and a sense of excitement, I began using PACE in my work; it was hard.

To begin with, it felt laboured. I had to consider every sentence, every word, every non-verbal response, and to consider it all carefully. And then to reconsider it. We are so used to thinking and responding in certain ways that we don't even think about it. It is just the way we are. But, like all habits, our responses can be changed. It just takes a bit of dedication.

One of the fundamentals of the PACE approach is to get to the bottom of things without ever using the word 'why'. Have a go; it is tricky to master. I spent many a journey to and from school practising model sentences without using 'why'.

I soon learned that the easiest way to get round the compulsion to ask 'why' was to simply echo whatever it was a child had said to me. For example, if a child came to me and said, 'Johnny hit me,' instead of my previous retort – 'Why do you think Johnny hit you?' – I would just say, 'Johnny hit you?' Note that I have rephrased it as a question.

I must warn you that, once you have tried this approach, it can become addictive. You see, when you repeat a child's words, something opens up within them and a dialogue is unleashed through which they explain the whole situation to you. Not only are you showing that you are listening to them, but also, over time, they start to take ownership of their actions and find solutions. I now have children who come up to me and, before we have even begun a conversation, they give me a full confession.

So simple and yet so powerful. You can use it with parents too, especially if you focus on acceptance and empathy.

6. HOW TO BUILD RELATIONSHIPS WITH PARENTS: PART I

Want to know the secret of building great working relationships with parents? Time.

The more time you can give to them – and yourself – the easier the job becomes. And this includes time beforehand to make sure that meetings go as successfully as possible. Making sure you are fully prepped is important, not only practically but also in terms of your frame of mind.

A top tip here is, whenever a parent asks for a meeting, find out there and then what it is they want to talk about. Sounds obvious, perhaps, but you will know that gut-wrenching feeling when a particular parent asks for a meeting. Forewarned is forearmed, you think, so you get the child's test results ready, you monitor their interactions with their peers and you add up all their house points, just to check they are in line with everyone else in the class. The day of the meeting arrives and, lo and behold, you sit down with the parent and find out they are considering taking the child to Australia for a family wedding and want to know what you think. All of that wasted time, effort and angst!

So, ask in advance and then prepare for the meeting you are going to have, not the one you think you are going to have.

7. HOW TO BUILD RELATIONSHIPS WITH PARENTS: PART II

Parents are our greatest ally. Give them our trust and time and, in return, they will educate us about their children. How empowering is that? Educating the educators. I even have amazing parents who will do research for me, digging out information to help me help their child. They care and they know I care. We all want the same thing, after all.

To get to this position, it is vital that we walk alongside our parents, especially when things are really difficult for them. I remember meeting a parent whose child had just joined our school. She told me that her child needed a high level of support for his additional needs – support the child wasn't receiving. 'We had been offered so much and given so little,' she explained, exasperated. I reassured her that I would help and, if I couldn't, I would find someone who could. It is a line I know she still quotes to this day. It was all she needed to hear (and it sends shivers down my spine every time I think about it). It was another defining eureka moment in my career as a SENDCO. Empathy and honesty working together seamlessly.

Working in this open way not only benefits parents, but it also allows us to reach that part of our common humanity which makes us want to help others – and we feel good when we do. Jamil Zaki, a professor of psychology at Stanford University, asserts in his 2019 book, *The War for Kindness*: 'Decades of evidence demonstrate that individuals who empathize with others also help themselves: attracting friends more easily, experiencing greater happiness, and suffering less depression than their less empathetic peers.'[2] Well, I will have a bit of that cherry pie, please.

Once we develop a strong connection with parents, we find ourselves in a wonderful symbiotic relationship with them, where everyone benefits in many ways. By flattening the hierarchy, with educators and parents working together, we create such a formidable and more often than not unstoppable force. And this is all the more important when we are dealing with outside agencies who can sniff out a chink in our armour at thirty paces. When they are faced by a single 'us' working collectively, they can't help but become part of that 'us' too.

---

2   J. Zaki, *The War for Kindness: Building Empathy in a Fractured World* (London: Robinson, 2019), p. 40.

8. SPIKY EMAILS FROM PARENTS

Have you ever received a combative email from a parent and felt personally attacked? How dare they?! Don't they know how much time you have spent trying to get that funding for their child? You have a good mind to …

First things first – breathe. Don't do anything now as it might make the situation worse. The most important thing as we tread our empathy road is to ensure that we continue building relationships of trust, respect and transparency for the long term and at all costs. That off-the-hip reply is probably not going to help.

Next up, consider the context in which they may be sending you the email. There is always more than one side to things, even spiky emails. It may well be that they are having a bad day. And don't go round grumbling to everyone about the message. That will only fuel your irritation, especially if the people you talk to agree with you. If you need to get it off your chest, make sure you speak to someone you trust, who will give you a balanced viewpoint and help you see the email from a different angle.

Once you have calmed down then, and only then, consider replying; however – and this is a big however – I would strongly suggest not replying by email. Pick up the phone instead or arrange a face-to-face discussion as soon as you possibly can. This maintains and builds that human connection and will lead to genuine dialogue. Emails flying backwards and forwards can make a battleground of your inbox where misconstrued words become the ammunition and the children can end up as collateral damage.

I know your heart will be beating hard as you make that call, but you will all feel better afterwards. All that is needed is a few minutes of bravery to ensure that trust and respect won't just be restored but strengthened in the long run.

I told you the job was hard!

9. BREAKING DOWN THE BARRIER BETWEEN TEACHERS AND PARENTS

I used to see the relationship between parents and teachers as a power struggle. One of us was right (me) and the other was wrong (them). One of the (many) downsides of such an approach is that it made me shy away from discussions and meetings. If I didn't meet with the parents, then I couldn't be proven wrong. Neat, eh?

Often, I simply didn't know what to do, and I considered owning up to that to be worse than ignoring the issue. As a consequence, parents would go straight to the head teacher to ask why I hadn't dealt with the situation. The upshot was two frustrated parents and an angry boss – and the problem was still there waiting for me.

I learned quickly that the only thing worse than having a meeting is not having a meeting. Without timely professional interactions, we see the very worst sort of snowball effect, where issues build up, stack up and become bigger in the process. I am not sure whether you can nip a snowball in the bud, but you get the idea.

I now know that saying 'I don't know' is far better than ignoring a situation. It is a professionally honest thing to say, 'I don't know, but I'm going to find out. Leave it with me and I'll get back in touch.' These words are a sign of strength, not weakness.

Remember, too, that the only thing worse than not saying 'I don't know' is pretending you do know when you don't. That way madness lies.

10. HOW DO PARENTS PERCEIVE SENDCOS?

How do your parents perceive your SENDCO role? Be honest. Do they see you as a giver of information? A sympathetic listener? A fountain of knowledge? An emotional crutch? Or all of the above?

If we are thought of as all those things, then we are definitely going to let them down at some stage. First and foremost, let the parents know that you are human, like them. You may not get it right all the time, but your aim is always to do the best for their children.

For example, when I put in for funding, we always know there is a chance that we will be unsuccessful. I make this clear to the parents from the outset. They need to know that I will try my best but, at the end of the day, I don't make the final decision; other people do. Depending on the result, I can be a shoulder to cry on, an ear to rant at or a source of ideas for what next, or a bit of all of them. We are all humans doing our best, and that best is better when we work together. When we are 'us', listening to and learning from each other.

The 'us' approach is very useful. Make it your goal in every interaction with a family. No hierarchy, no ego, no fudging. It all adds up. I was told the other day that I don't 'fob people off'. I will take that; it means I am doing things right. I think I will have that on my gravestone: 'Here lies Ginny Bootman. SENDCO. She didn't fob people off.' Nice!

11. REMEMBER, WE ARE JUST PASSING THROUGH

A colleague once said something that still resonates with me: 'We are transient in the lives of children with additional needs.'

Think about it: that child whose special needs fill your head, your meeting schedule and your planner for a few years. The family have a whole lifetime behind them and a longer one ahead. Our role, then, isn't just about firefighting and sorting things out in the here and now. There is a long-term project underway. We might have our empathy road, but the family's road is long and winding indeed. It makes me feel emotional just writing those words.

Through our strength, we can help parents to be strong themselves. Through our listening, we can make sure they are heard. Through our voice, we can help them to find their own voice. The greatest gifts I give to the families with whom I work are the stepping stones they need as they move towards secondary education. These stones aren't just procedural or administrative (although there is a lot of that involved, especially when you act as the interface between the family and the local authority). They are also about helping parents to find the strength they need for the (sadly inevitable) fight they will face to ensure their child receives the education they deserve.

12. HOME AND SCHOOL – STRONGER TOGETHER

Strength is a two-way thing. The closer you are working with a family, the more you are an 'us' and the stronger you will be. Once, during an important meeting, the outside agents involved couldn't believe how in tune home and school were as a team. We were literally finishing each other's sentences.

One side effect of this closeness is that I can get emotional during meetings. I am a caring human; ergo, I am a passionate one. I once attended a meeting when I was being cross-examined in front of outside agents and parents. I knew that what I said would have a long-term impact on the child's future, which is quite some responsibility. That is a lasting legacy. I knew that every word I uttered was being analysed, but I also knew the parents were with me 100%. And this unity won the day.

How did we make this happen? It all goes back to trust and transparency. What was said in that meeting were my words, but they expressed what we all firmly and passionately believed in for that child. The words were simply an extension of many previous conversations. There was nothing new, no surprises, just a common dialogue.

13. IT ISN'T PERSONAL

Can you remember a time when something happened in your life and you became really annoyed and took it out on those you love? Of course you can – you are human. Parents are human too, and as a caring SENDCO you might well be in the firing line for something that isn't your fault. The system has failed them (again), for whatever reason, and suddenly you are facing blowback from the fallen house of cards. We always hurt the ones we love, after all.

Often, the SENDCO is the person that angry and frustrated parents get in touch with because what they really need is our help, guidance and support – not to mention an ear and a shoulder. With passions running high, this can sometimes come across in a clumsy manner; don't react. Pause, breathe and then put on their shoes and take a stroll down the empathy road. How would you react if you had received (more) bad news about your child's education? They know that you are there for them, that you won't judge and that you will always listen.

Then there are the parents whom you barely know but who have a go at you. The thing to remember here is that what is really happening is they are stress testing you. They are sussing you out to check whether you are good enough for their child. When you see things in this way, it changes the nature of the interaction, doesn't it? You need to rise to the challenge and prove yourself.

And, believe me, they will keep on testing you and you will keep on proving yourself.

14. MAKE TRIPS WORK FOR EVERYONE, INCLUDING PARENTS

I went on a school trip recently. A large part of the day involved climbing trees so we could zip-wire back down again. Such fun! A large proportion of the days before the trip was spent planning and communicating with the parents of our SEND children.

It wasn't just a question of risk assessments, although we did a great deal of them and in considerable detail. We also planned and over-planned. Everything was covered and discussed with staff and parents alike (who was going on the bus, who was meeting us there, who was scared of heights, etc.).

In the end, we had more one-to-one support than we needed but, hey, it is better to over-plan than under-plan. The majority of the children didn't need access to the systems we had in place 'just in case' – the extra snacks, drinks, ear defenders and sensory toys – but we were ready. We had been in email contact with all our parents of children with additional needs, sharing the risk assessment, explaining the day and our contingencies, informing them which group their child would be in, enabling them to ask questions and make suggestions (they know their child better than anyone) – questions we answered and suggestions we took on board wherever we could. It was a lot of work, but it made for a calm, successful, inclusive and stress-free trip for everyone (if you don't include zip-wiring out of a tree).

15. THE SMALL THINGS PARENTS TELL US ARE, IN FACT, THE BIG THINGS

Next time a parent speaks to you, listen out for the small things. These are so often the things that make the biggest difference. When a parent begins a sentence with, 'I know you're really busy but ...' or 'This probably isn't anything but ...' my ears prick up, my SENDCO sense tingles and I listen more carefully than ever. As I have focused on building trust with the parents, I know that they are more likely to open up, and that openness often comes in the guise of little throwaway lines.

For example, I recently had a meeting with parents and, as always, I was wrapping things up with my usual, 'Is there anything else you would like to discuss?' question. The 'Well, there is one little thing ...' response led to a deep-level discussion about an aspect of their child which I wasn't expecting to find out about. The moral of this story is two-fold. Firstly, always make space for the little things that end up being big things. Secondly, parents can tell us very personal big things and at unexpected times, so be ready for how you will react. Your reaction will have implications for your future meetings.

16. FOLLOW THE EMPATHY ROAD

Imagine the scene. You are visiting an Empathy Museum. Inside, you are wearing headphones through which you are listening to a recording of an interview with a stranger. They are talking about their life. While you are listening, you are walking around the museum in their shoes.

This scenario, a real-life art installation displayed in both Britain and Australia by artist Clare Patey, is described in Peter Bazalgette's 2017 book, *The Empathy Instinct*. It is called 'A Mile in My Shoes', and is part of the museum's ambition to be 'an experiential arts space dedicated to helping us all look at the world through other people's eyes'.[3]

There, in an arty nutshell, is the professional life of the committed SENDCO. When we follow the empathy road, we imagine ourselves walking in the shoes of the parents with whom we work. I often put on my metaphorical headphones and listen to the story behind the child. It is a powerful thing to do and will reveal tremendous stores of patience and empathy that you didn't know you had.

---

3   P. Bazalgette, *The Empathy Instinct: How to Create A More Civil Society* (London: John Murray, 2017), p. 253.

17. SORRY SEEMS TO BE THE HARDEST WORD

How often, as teachers, do we say, 'I was wrong and I am sorry' – and really mean it too? I have always found it curious how many people think saying sorry means they are losing power, credibility or respect, or all three. How wrong can we be by not admitting when we are wrong?

Saying that we have made a mistake means we are showing our all-important human side. What is more, we are mirroring to the children that it is okay to get things wrong and that it is important to say we were wrong, to say we are sorry and (this is the bit I love) to say, 'I will try really hard not to do it again.' That is the human part of us. Nobody can be sure they won't make the same mistake again, but at least we can try our hardest not to.

Have a go at saying you are sorry or you were wrong in your classroom setting and see how the children react. It is an interesting experiment. (And remember, 'Sorry' is one word. It is never 'Sorry but …') When I first started apologising, the children were a little taken aback. But I soon saw the difference it made. They became much more ready to say they were sorry for something they had done.

Children mirror what they see around them, so be aware of how you are behaving. Honesty works in the same way too. When I admit how awful my drawing is, but still try anyway, they become my best cheerleaders, appreciating my honesty and encouraging me for trying.

18. HUMOUR IS A HUMAN CONNECTOR

How often do we use humour in the classroom? And how often do we laugh at ourselves? Not enough maybe.

Let me give you an example. I was in my classroom trying to use a touchscreen to connect to the interactive whiteboard. Suddenly, a quiet voice said, 'Mrs Bootman, that isn't an iPad – it's a laptop. Touching the screen won't help! You need to use your mouse.' When it comes to learning to laugh at myself and build rapport with my children, technology is an important source of inspiration. I bet it is for you too.

In a similar vein, I was getting frustrated for forever losing the interactive whiteboard pen (this piece of equipment is clearly my Achilles' heel!). After a whole-class search, it would be found on top of a cupboard or among the glue sticks or some such random place. It was only after a few weeks of this pantomime that a child approached me politely at the end of one lesson and explained, 'Mrs Bootman, you do know you can just use your finger instead of the pen on the board, don't you?' An hallelujah moment and another laugh to cement a relationship with that child.

Being human means being vulnerable, and being vulnerable means laughing at yourself sometimes. The more human you can appear, the better your connection with the children, especially those who feel most vulnerable themselves.

19. THE POWER OF THE THIRD PERSON

I once had a child in my class who wouldn't own up to any of the misdemeanours that I knew, he knew and we all knew he had committed. Every accusation was met with a flat, knee-jerk denial. For whatever reason, he didn't have the capacity to acknowledge he had done anything wrong. Something needed to change. It was then that I came across what I call 'the third-person approach'.

I asked him to choose a Lego figure – let's call him Mr B – and from then on, if there had been an incident in the playground, we would both ask this figure if he had anything to tell us. 'Did you, Mr B, do anything you perhaps shouldn't have during playtime today?' It was as if I had administered a truth pill! The Lego figure was able to tell me in great detail everything that had happened in the playground and what was behind it. He was also able to take guidance about what should have happened. Interestingly, Mr B was also able to accept sanctions – something he and the child underwent together, of course.

I found this whole approach and its success really interesting at first. Then it became even more fascinating and insightful. The child decided that from now on Mr B would have the same name as himself. In this way, we could explore tricky situations with the child referring to himself in the third person. He was then, even more directly, able to accept responsibility and ownership for his actions and explain to his Lego self what he should do next time to ensure the incident wasn't repeated.

I love how this approach unlocks the child's ability to take ownership of their actions, something that is vital for them to learn and move on. It is a strategy I still use because it allows a degree of space between a child and their actions, which enables us to explore what has happened in a non-threatening way.

You can use a similar strategy when encouraging children to recognise and understand the feelings and actions of others. I find that they will often empathise more with a character in a book, for example, than another individual in their class. By using stories richly interwoven with the possibility of empathy, children's ability to step into someone else's shoes can be developed. I often use *The Miraculous Journey of Edward Tulane* by Kate DiCamillo.[4] It is a story about a lost toy rabbit, and I have a toy rabbit in the classroom while we read the book. When the children are reading, the rabbit sits next to them and they talk to it about how it might be feeling. I have found this to be a powerful way to help children build connection, especially those who may find it difficult to identify with others.

20. PLAY DETECTIVE

A colleague shared with me that a child in her class was fine working at their workstation, but when asked to go and sit at a table, something shifted and their work and behaviour deteriorated. Following the empathy road means that we explore what is happening, not to find out what the child is doing wrong and fixing it, but discover-

---

4   K. DiCamillo, *The Miraculous Journey of Edward Tulane* (London: Walker Books, 2006).

ing what that child is feeling when faced with that classroom transition. We literally put ourselves in detective mode.

While chatting with the child in a non-threatening way, he revealed that he felt safe at his workstation, but when faced with having to choose a chair to sit on at a table, he felt overwhelmed. It wasn't the transition that was causing the problem but the element of choice! We came up with the idea of assigning the child a particular chair at a particular table. In this way, whenever the children had to find a chair, he would know that he could always go to the same chair.

I checked in with my colleague a week later. The child was now much less stressed and his behaviour and work were of a consistently high standard. He was also much happier and more confident because he no longer had to worry about choosing. Such a simple thing to fix, but one we could only get to through empathy, understanding and a bit of detective work.

Playing detective and looking closely at a situation through an empathetic magnifying glass often helps us to find simple answers to even the hardest-to-crack problems. Another example was a child who found break times really challenging. She complained that her peers were invading her space. After a discussion with her parents, we found out that she had a real love for Lego. A box of Lego was provided by home, which she took out at break times and found like-minded friends who wanted to join her in a world of construction. Case solved. It was the child in the playground with a box of Lego, not Colonel Mustard in the library with a lead pipe, after all.

21. CHOOSE YOUR WORDS CAREFULLY

Words matter; with some children, they matter even more. As a SENDCO, it is vital that you think about what you say and that you are ready for whatever reaction your words provoke, regardless of how you mean them or what you thought you said.

Picture the scene. I have the job of sorting out who is on today's school bus, so I make the innocuous request, bus register in hand, 'Please put your hand up if you're on the bus.' Five hands go up. The register, however, tells me there are only four on the bus today. Identifying the mistaken child, I point out that he will be on the bus tomorrow but not today, to which he replies, 'I know, but you asked us to put up our hands if we were on the bus. And I am. Tomorrow.'

I know now that I needed to make it clear I was asking about today specifically and thanked him for helping me. 'That's okay, Miss,' he replied, happy to have helped. Our tone is as vital as the words we say. The child felt valued throughout our discussion because what he said had been acknowledged.

Make your words clear and be ready for the fact that, no matter how precise you think you are being, there is nearly always room for misconceptions and misinterpretations to creep in.

22. DON'T CONFRONT, COMFORT

A child is what might be described as 'kicking off' in your class. Now what? Our instinct is often to move in and do whatever is necessary – quieten, pacify, threaten, bribe or reprimand – to bring calm back to a fraught situation. When you apply the PACE approach (described in tips 4 and 5), what you do next should create a sense of safety for all those involved.

Faced with this situation a few years ago, I employed *acceptance* as a starting point for my response. What I needed to accept first and foremost was that this child needed space, so that is what I gave him. From a distance I quietly said, 'You are safe.' After a few moments, I asked if I could step a little closer towards him. If he said no, then I accepted that and waited, repeating the words, 'You are safe.' Eventually, and calmly, the child let me know when he was happy for me to approach him.

Teachers often want quick fixes. They want to know what to do when A, B or C happens, and how to make it stop happening quickly and effectively. I get that. However, approaches that have empathy at their heart are not quick-fix solutions. They are a way of being, not a way of just doing. The empathy road is long and winding. It is a road you tread day in, day out, month in, month out. It is part of who you are, not a mask you wear.

When the children see that you are consistent in your approach, you begin to break down their barriers and connections are made. You connect with them at a deeper level and are therefore much better equipped to help them. What is more, they learn to walk the empathy road themselves. Calmly and consistently, you show them how beneficial such a route is for everyone. When they stumble off the path – which they will (we all will) – they know they will always be able to get back on.

All roads have bumps and even potholes. Children need to understand that behaviour has consequences. Empathy doesn't mean that children whose conduct falls outside of the school rules are never reprimanded or sanctioned. Far from it. This bothered me at first, as I worried that if I sanctioned children I would lose their hard-won trust. Interestingly, it turned out that they accepted the sanction – the bump in the road – with equanimity and resilience because we had addressed what happened in an empathetic way. And then we all moved on.

23. THE POWER OF THE PRE-MEETING: PART I – PARENTS

Recently, I had an important SEND meeting with a parent and outside agents. The mother asked me for a pre-meeting. I know – that is like two meetings for the price of one. What busy professional would want to double their workload like that? It is easy to try and put them off, but what was bothering her in the build-up to the main meeting was letting me down and letting her child down. She was worried that her voice wasn't going to be heard in the meeting and she was scared of not getting the outcome her child needed – and that it would be her fault.

Of course, I had a pre-meeting with her. We sat down together over a cuppa (if there isn't tea, it isn't a meeting) and had a really good chat. When she left, she knew I would be her voice in the meeting if necessary. But, with the pressure off, it will come as no surprise that she positively shone among all those professionals.

We recognise how vulnerable some parents feel in important meetings, so knowing that a fellow human being is ready and willing to speak up for you, if necessary, provides a great safety net. It unleashes all sorts of confidence in a parent. So many meetings have a sense of make or break/ now or never looming over them, which can get to a seasoned professional like me, so imagine how a stressed parent might feel. While some people are happy for you to communicate on their behalf, for others, your support means they have the confidence to talk openly.

And when they do speak up and speak out, the wins are so much more significant, even if the outcome of the meeting goes against us, that time …

24. THE POWER OF THE PRE-MEETING: PART II – STAFF

Parents aren't the only ones who can benefit from meeting before a meeting. Increasingly, I am getting together with colleagues before we go on to meet with parents. In this way, we can make sure we are of the same opinion, and if we discover we aren't, we can find a way to make sure we are before the actual meeting takes place.

This was a lesson hard won, years ago, after being in a meeting where a colleague came up with something as unhelpful as it was unexpected. As you know you all want the same thing, you assume that you will go about it in the same way, but you may have made a dodgy assumption about what that 'same thing' really is. Your ideal outcomes and fallback compromise might be different from those of your head teacher or the child's class teacher, so have a pre-meeting to prevent this from happening. It gets those disagreements or misconceptions out of the way, so that everyone is speaking the same language.

Generally, your pre-meetings will focus on items such as outside involvement, funding and timetabling. Once you have discussed and agreed on these matters, there will be no surprises – at least, not from your side of the meeting. Moreover, there will be occasions when all the interested parties from the school can't make the meeting due to simple logistics. A pre-meeting means that all voices are heard, all views are gathered and everyone has their say.

I also recommend making your parents aware that these pre-meetings have taken place. It shows a real commitment to the child in question, which will be of benefit further down the line, and they will be reassured that everyone who works with their child has been part of an important dialogue.

25. THE WHY, WHEN, WHERE AND WHO OF A MEETING: PART I

You have got an important meeting with a parent coming up. The *when* has been agreed, as has the *who*, and now you are more than a little preoccupied with the *why*. But, if you are genuinely following the empathy road, then there is another question you need to consider carefully – *where*?

From deep within the shoes of the parent you are about to meet, where would be the best place to assemble? Is that office too formal and imposing? Is that set-up across the table too confrontational? Are those tiny Year 4 chairs really the best seating option? Think about the options that will give the meeting the best possible chance of succeeding.

Maybe the classroom, suitably arranged, is the best place, or maybe it isn't? What about the staffroom – coffee tables and comfy/comfier chairs might be better, as well as being closer to a kettle and the biscuit tin? Being more public might have its uses too. And what about outside, weather permitting, on neutral territory? I have had summer-term meetings in an open pergola in the school grounds, and it gave the occasion a much needed sense of calmness.

Whenever I can, I will give the parents a choice about where they would like to meet. A word of warning, though – if you give options, you have to be happy with whatever they choose. It isn't a great start if you go into a meeting resenting their choice.

Post-pandemic, we are all more used to having our meetings online. This may well suit busy parents or those for whom coming into the school environment might be problematic or triggering. Don't assume anything, though. I was recently lining up an online meeting when my SENDCO senses started tingling and I realised the parent wasn't comfortable with a virtual meeting. By quickly offering a face-to-face option instead, I was paving the way for what turned out to be a very positive meeting, one that most probably wouldn't have had such a good outcome if I had simply offered an online meeting.

26. THE WHY, WHEN, WHERE AND WHO OF A MEETING: PART II

How often do we set up a meeting for right at the end of the school day? On one hand, it makes sense, but on the other, being part of an important meeting when you are feeling wrung out from a busy day means you might not get the best out of yourself or your colleagues.

Or what about squeezing that vital meeting into lunch-time? For me, lunchtime is about eating your sandwiches and having a chat. If the meeting is supposed to be important, then rushing through it might not be the right thing to do.

As before, ask the other attendees what time would suit them best without assuming anything. You might find time during the day or before school starts that is mutually convenient. With the flexibility that online meetings bring these days, I often suggest a Zoom call at 5pm, by which time most people can get home, have a cuppa and feel that little bit calmer and less fraught. Of course, set a time limit for a meeting this close to the end of the working day, and make sure you stick to it.

27. WHY ARE WE HAVING THE MEETING?

I mentioned earlier how important it is to make sure everyone knows what the meeting is about, and not to just assume, so there are no surprises and people can come fully prepared. I find that when everyone knows its purpose, there is more chance that people will have considered the content prior to the meeting. Everyone will have had time to think things through beforehand, and there is less likelihood of coming to rash or badly thought-through decisions.

For example, I recently had a meeting booked in and, prior to it taking place, I received an email outlining possible solutions to the discussion points we would be covering. Without pre-empting the decisions to be taken when we did meet, we could consider the various options in advance, which helped to ensure that the meeting itself was efficient, smooth and productive.

28. THE ROAD TO NOWHERE

Have you ever been to one of those meetings when the conversation seems to be going round in circles with no definite end in sight? One way to break this cycle is to agree that the issue in hand needs more time, so a further meeting will be convened at a later date once everyone has had an opportunity to let the matter percolate.

Usually, when the follow-up meeting happens, the answer that was eluding us originally is quickly found and agreed upon. It does mean we end up with two meetings, but both were as purposeful as possible. Much better than one meeting with its infinite loop.

29. THE LIVE AGENDA

I am still amazed how few people have heard of the idea of creating a live agenda before a meeting, let alone actually using this great approach.

The way it works is to create a shared document listing the planned agenda but with an extra column next to each item where anyone can add notes prior to the meeting. It becomes a 'living' document and ensures that everyone comes to the meeting ready and prepared. Furthermore, people can add to the agenda in advance, thus avoiding that sinking feeling we all get when someone suddenly raises two new points under 'any other business' when everyone really just wants to go home.

A live agenda also means you can hit the pause button on certain items, if necessary, without offending anyone, as it is clear that you will allocate time and come back to it in a future meeting. Finally, the agenda can be used as the minutes of the meeting, which also saves time and effort.

30. HOW LONG SHOULD A MEETING LAST (AND CAN WE HAVE A CUPPA)?

I try not to organise meetings that last any longer than an hour. In my experience, people start losing focus if it goes on longer than that. Knowing when a meeting will end – and knowing this will be adhered to – creates a nice little parcel for everyone concerned, especially when it is bundled up with the why, when, where and who we discussed in tips 25 and 26.

To ensure the meeting sticks to the time limit, it can help to send out information electronically beforehand. In this way, you come together to discuss the content, not to meet it for the first time. There is nothing worse than having information read out to you – other than, heaven forbid, walking into a meeting and finding someone ready with a set of PowerPoint slides.

My most successful meetings with colleagues usually entail one of us bringing an idea – or the beginnings of an idea – and then exploring, editing and refining the idea together, never losing sight of our focus on helping the children in our care.

Also, anyone who knows me knows that I always strongly suggest they bring a cuppa along to the meeting. Coming together around a cup of tea gives meetings a very different feel; more like a relaxed but focused conversation than anything too formal or stuffy.

31. WHO SHOULD COME TO THE MEETING?

Ever had one of those 'Duh!' moments during a meeting when you realise that you haven't invited someone whose input you really could do with? Making sure the right people are present is vital, but it is something we can get wrong from time to time. To avoid ending up having another meeting after your first meeting (and undermining the person who should have been invited), have a proper think about who needs to be there and, equally importantly, who doesn't. It can be frustrating to clear a whole hour for a meeting only to find that you were needed for a five-minute slot or that receiving the minutes via email would have been a much better use of your time.

The questions to ask are: who needs to be there for the whole meeting, and are you sure? Who needs to be there for part of the meeting, and are you sure? Who could get by with just having the live agenda and the minutes electronically, and are you sure? As well as the all-important question, do you need the meeting at all?

32. THE POWER OF THE POP-UP MEETING (AND WHEN NOT TO DO IT)

As a SENDCO, it can be easy to let class teachers do the meet and greet at the beginning and end of the school day, but this is golden impromptu SENDCO meeting time, so get out there and get chatting!

Talk to the parents you don't know as well as the ones you do. Talk to any and all of them. Chat about the weather, what they are wearing, what their child is wearing, what you wish you were wearing. Start those conversations, and before you know it the conversations will start themselves. Be known as the member of staff who talks to anyone and everyone. Why? Because in this way you will become known as someone who is approachable. Parents will be far more willing to open up to you about the bigger things when they know they can talk to you about the smaller things.

Whatever you do, don't go out to have *that* chat, which isn't fair on the parent or child. If there is an 'I'm afraid we need to talk about Kevin' conversation to be had, make sure you get in touch with the parent beforehand and invite them into school, so you can have a sensible conversation in the right conditions and without other parents watching on or listening in.

33. DRESS TO IMPRESS

What you are wearing speaks before you have even opened your mouth. The clothes you opt for at the beginning of the day not only send a message to you (for example, I wear bright colours if I want to feel more confident or to cheer myself up) but also to others. So, what would you like your clothes to say on your behalf?

If I want to come across as the consummate professional and ensure I am listened to, I might choose a black outfit. For me, dark colours signify that I mean business, and that is as relevant for me to hear as the people I am meeting. I am not trying to scare anyone, but I am sending the message that I have something important to say. I find this especially useful in meetings that involve outside agencies where some professionals may not realise just how good us SENDCOs are.

Of course, sometimes a black outfit might make me blend in a little too much or appear unapproachable, so this is when I choose something from the flowery end of the sartorial spectrum. I have been through two inspections recently (working across more than one school) and on both occasions a floral dress has helped me to feel comfortable and confident. Those of you who know me from Twitter will also know how proud I am of my ruby red 'Dorothy' shoes, which completed the look on both occasions. Instant confidence when I needed it the most!

Why not brighten up your outfit with a colourful tie or scarf, or wear that suit which makes you stand out? Find your inner confidence through colour, and let me know how you get on.

34. HOW DO STAFF PERCEIVE THE SENDCO?

'Do this or you can say goodbye to your glue sticks,' probably isn't the best way to develop a healthy working relationship with your class teachers, but I have seen this corrosive approach all too often. Like an empathetic Terminator, we present recommendations and instructions from the educational psychologist with an attitude that says, 'Do it like this, or else *I'll be back*,' and then we wonder why the child isn't making as much progress as any of us would have hoped.

Some of this pressure comes from the expectations we put on ourselves, believing that the message from the professionals is that we must implement all their recommendations by the following day. Not only is this inaccurate but it is also damaging to even try.

The important thing to remember here is what the CO in SENDCO stands for. Our job isn't to lead and insist but to *coordinate*, to bring disparate professionals together successfully and effectively around the needs of the children for whom we all want so much. If I am being honest, it has taken me a while to get to this understanding.

I remember how hard it was initially to hand over any responsibility for addressing a child's needs to their teacher and to trust them to get it right. This approach makes no sense, though. There are so many of them (teachers, parents, children) and so few of us. I know now that the SENDCO's primary role in interactions with class teachers is to provide them with valuable information, which they can filter and sift in order to make the best possible decisions about the care and education of the children in their class. After all, they know the children far better than we do.

What information might they need to be in the best position to help a child? And how can we provide them with that information in a timely, flexible and accessible way? These are the questions we really need to be asking as SENDCOs.

Once we grasp this important principle, we will stop making promises to parents that aren't ours to keep. We can't promise a parent that something will happen, in the same way that we can't make a teacher do something. As a class teacher, I experienced the 'dumping of strategies you must implement and, no, you have no extra support to achieve it' approach, and it just gets my back up. It isn't helpful when we are trying to walk the empathy road.

When in doubt, the golden rule of empathy helps: do unto others as you would have them do unto you. Ask yourself, could I do what I am expecting someone else to do? If it is a 'no', or even 'I'm not sure', it is time for a rethink.

35. BROADENING HORIZONS

Have you ever considered utilising your SENDCO knowledge and experience with a wider audience of teachers? I have worked with teachers in alternative provision and specialist settings, with secondary SENDCOs and also lectured PGCE students about SEND. All of us want the same for the children in our care, and by broadening my audience, I am dispelling the myths others may have regarding SEND. It is a great way to spread positivity about special needs.

36. HOW TO ENSURE STAFF TRAINING SESSIONS ARE AVAILABLE TO ALL

Have you ever led a training session only to find out, just as you are about to start, that some teachers haven't been able to attend? This often occurs when classes have job shares and one of the teachers isn't working that day. It can be a soul-destroying way to begin.

One way round this is to record the session and then save it on a shared drive. You can then signpost people to the resource and ask them to watch it at a time that is convenient for them. You can even give them a time code for when a particularly relevant part of the training takes place.

Not only does this save you from having to rerun the training, but it also means that those who did attend can revisit the learning as and when necessary. I have had very positive feedback from doing this, so I would recommend giving it a whirl.

37. CLASS TEACHERS ARE THE EXPERTS WHEN IT COMES TO THEIR CHILDREN

As SENDCOs, we are always busy. If you are anything like me, you spend a great deal of your time filling in paperwork, chasing referrals, making tea, filling in more paperwork, contacting parents, making more tea, contacting outside agencies and making tea. If we aren't careful, we can be in our office for the majority of our time. We SENDCOs need to make a conscious decision to leave our offices on a regular basis and get into the classrooms to see the children with whom we are working.

The staff I work with really appreciate me doing observations, not to give them solutions but to reassure them that what they are doing is great. They also value having another pair of eyes in the room, helping them see things through a different lens.

It is important to spend time with the teacher after an observation. Do this as soon as you both possibly can, ideally straight after the lesson. Sit down with the teacher and talk through what you have observed, giving recommendations along with your feedback. You aren't an inspector or their line manager, so this process should involve a positive and constructive conversation and the teacher shouldn't feel wary about being judged.

I also need to remember that I am not the class teacher. My recommendations might be useful, but they might be impractical for that teacher. If all my suggestions aren't adopted, that is fine. In general, I anticipate that 50% of the recommendations I propose will be used, with the other 50% simply not practical within the context of that particular classroom. I don't expect teachers to justify to me why they aren't doing what I have suggested because I trust them completely. I know they will implement systems if they can; and if they can't, there is a good reason why.

My teachers know I am always available to talk things through with them, but, they are the class teacher and my role is to advise and guide, not tell them what to do.

38. VALUING ALL THE STAFF WHO WORK WITH OUR CHILDREN

Do you invite the teaching assistant who works with particular children to SEND meetings? Or do you think it is unnecessary or even inappropriate?

Colleagues have told me that expecting teaching assistants to attend important meetings can put them in a difficult position – for example, if a parent asks them a question they are unable to answer. My response here is always the same: we are a team and we attend meetings as a team. The teaching assistant will have a perspective on the child that is different and useful, so they should have the chance to speak up. Furthermore, I have had review meetings where parents have asked for the teaching assistant to be present.

The role of the teaching assistant must never be belittled or overlooked. These key staff members need to feel comfortable liaising with parents, knowing that you and the class teacher have got their back. Some teaching assistants may feel uncomfortable attending meetings or may be unable to do so, and that is fine too. When they can't be present, ask them to submit their views and insights in written form in advance, as appropriate.

Similarly, some teaching assistants are happy to communicate with parents via home–school books, whereas others may be more reluctant if they are worried about how this may be viewed by parents. One way I have managed this situation as a class teacher is to work alongside the teaching assistant on home–school books, perhaps editing an email together prior to sending it home.

39. SENDCO SURGERIES

One SENDCO I met told me about the SENDCO surgery she ran. At a set time each week, any member of staff who wanted to talk about anything special needs related could pop in for a chat. She had also set up an online version via Zoom, so anyone could drop in while the surgery was open. If no one did stop by, either in person or virtually, that was also fine. The SENDCO just got on with her work and no time had been wasted.

40. DON'T JUDGE A BOOK BY ITS COVER – READ A FEW CHAPTERS FIRST

When we first meet people, it is natural to form an opinion quickly. It is also very easy for this judgement to be wrong.

Recently, I met a teacher who seemed very anxious about a child in her class. She was keen for me to help her with the child, and within minutes of meeting her she was asking for my advice. On the face of it, she seemed to lack confidence with respect to giving the child the support they needed. Alarm bells started ringing.

What I thought I was seeing was evidence of a child not being fully supported in their classroom setting, and that this was a situation that needed to be addressed urgently. The teacher wanted to know when the funding application was coming through, and she seemed keen to stress that she was unable to move on the child's learning until this funding was in place.

It was as if a tsunami had hit me. A teacher lacking the professional skill set needed to work with a child with special needs, and the child not receiving the support they sorely needed. What should I do to fix this?

Firstly, I needed to breathe, and then speak to another member of staff who worked alongside the teacher. I needed to go beyond my first impressions. When I did, it transpired that I was witnessing a teacher who cared deeply about her children and who was simply not acknowledging the amazing work she was already doing with the child. In fact, it became clear that she was a teacher with an instinctive grasp of SEND who didn't know how effective she was being, which is a very different conclusion to the one to which I had jumped.

It was an important lesson for me in not judging a book by its cover (and in breathing). Make sure you have conversations with everyone involved in supporting a child, so you understand properly the assistance that is being provided – the mantra of 'seek first to understand'. By taking the time to understand the staff with whom we work as individuals, we can get to know their special skills and help them to understand what an incredible job they are doing. Praise and support, not judgement, then become the norm.

41. THREE TYPES OF TEACHER

When I first meet staff, they generally fall into three categories. Now, I know this a broad generalisation, but bear with me and my experience on this.

Firstly, we have the 'I need help. I need a teaching assistant full time. I can't do anything for Johnny unless you give me an extra pair of hands in the classroom!' teacher.

Secondly, there is the 'I don't need any help. I've got it all sorted. Whatever you suggest I'll ignore and, instead, follow my tried-and-tested route because that's how I do it. End of!' teacher.

Finally, there is the 'I've tried this. Can we sit down and talk about it and come up with a plan together?' teacher.

Of course, the teacher we all long for is the third type, but to get there takes investment and trust from everyone involved. Positive and professional collaboration doesn't happen overnight. As with any stage on the empathy road, there are bumps, blocks and 'road ahead closed' signs along the way.

The best way to navigate the road is by being honest, authentic and transparent. I don't have all of the answers, no one does, but I can at least make sure my colleagues are aware of what I do know. I have learned to build some great working relationships in this way.

In my experience, the staff who fall into the first and second teacher types do so out of fear, a perceived lack of time and that horrible (but understandable) feeling that they have to choose between helping a child with additional needs or supporting the rest of the class. By understanding these very real concerns and addressing them head on, you can start to navigate past these blocks. This is when their resistance starts to ebb away and their shoulders relax – and I put the kettle on.

42. THE TRAFFIC LIGHT SYSTEM

One way I find useful for thinking about the stages a teacher may be at in their approach to supporting children with additional needs is through a traffic light analogy.

If the teacher is seeing red, the challenges of supporting children with additional needs has hijacked their professional brain. They are scared of the implications for themselves, for their class and for the school as a whole.

Amber is where you get to through careful and empathetic discussion. Now, they are starting to get a better idea of the logistics, the staffing and the true (not simply perceived) implications for them and their class.

Green is go – let's do this! And we will do it together. When things don't work out, when we hit that pothole in the empathy road and end up on the hard shoulder of bitter disillusionment, we will work together to find a solution. As ever, honest and timely communication is right at the heart of things.

43. BREAK IT DOWN TO BUILD IT UP

One of the best pieces of SEND paperwork I have ever devised was a breakdown of the school day into ten-minute slots. I gave this to the staff to see when teaching assistants were working with individual children and to pinpoint where there were gaps in the day and where extra support was needed. Teachers could also use it to identify how much one-to-one time individual children were receiving throughout the week, plan timetables and determine where there were opportunities for further interventions to take place.

Interestingly, no one felt micro-managed because it was a tool for teachers to look at their own timetables. It was also a starting point for teachers to come and chat with me about their timetables, not the other way round. Ownership is so important.

44. HOW TO SUPPORT THE CLASS TEACHER

It is a fine line: one minute you are merrily supporting a class teacher and the next you are in danger of undermining them. SENDCOs walk this line on a daily basis.

This line is always in the forefront of my mind when I contact parents. For example, I have learned to always 'cc' class teachers into my emails to parents, and they do the same to me. This means there are no unwelcome surprises when a parent comments about something that either I or the class teacher have spoken about. To 'cc' rather than 'bcc' keeps the communication transparent, so everyone knows who is part of the conversation, and stands us in good stead for future dialogue.

Another way of walking the line is simply to listen. Sometimes a teacher just wants to talk about their class. They aren't looking for interventions or advice; they just need an expert ear. I have found that good teachers always think they should be doing more for their children. Listening to a teacher express their concerns and ambitions for their class allows them to see just how much they are doing, especially when you can commend them for doing such a great job. Offering advice and suggestions about how they can make small, manageable changes to make things even better (without loads of extra work) has its place, but choose your moment. Sometimes an empathetic ear is all that is needed.

45. WHO LIAISES WITH PARENTS WHEN?

Flowcharts are great but invisible ones are even better. I have a decision tree in my head to help me remember who is the right person to liaise with parents and when they should be doing it. Why? In the past, I have inadvertently jumped in too soon to talk to parents about issues when, in the first instance at least, that conversation should have been with the class teacher. Acting too soon means we can end up undermining the teacher, which isn't good for anyone. Make sure you are always considering who is the best first port of call and that this is clearly communicated to all concerned.

This 'who says what when' element of the flowchart works in both directions: equally, the class teacher can't speak for the SENDCO. Once you have built positive working relationships with your colleagues, they will know when and how to bring you into the process of communicating with parents. If a teacher asks me to attend a meeting with parents, more often than not it will be because they want me there for a specific reason, perhaps for support or to answer questions pertaining to particular aspects of SEND about which I have more knowledge.

I recently started attending parents' evenings. It is a really useful way to hear class teachers talking about the children in their class, such that a much more focused and purposeful dialogue between the class teacher, parents and myself can follow. It is also a privilege to hear my colleagues speaking about the children in their care.

46. MANAGING OUR TIME EFFECTIVELY

As a SENDCO across four primary schools – and working purely as a SENDCO – I am fortunate that my time is flexible. Not being classroom based means my timetable is in my own hands. The staff I work with really appreciate this flexibility, as they can speak to me about a child in their class at a time that suits them best. For some, this is after school; for others, it is in their planning time during the school day.

Our new-found expertise and confidence in the virtual world also means I don't have to be in the building for these meetings. Chatting online brings a whole new dimension to this flexibility.

It isn't just about online conversations either. Using interactive platforms to share and edit documents has been a revolutionary aspect of our virtual meetings. It gives us all the chance to create and view important documents during the meeting and edit them together live. My colleagues have commented on numerous occasions how great it is to be able to revise documents together in this way. It means we can all use our time wisely and productively, go through a process together in real time, and all see and agree on the end result.

Working in more than one school means that I carry everything I need in my briefcase, which in its simplest terms means an iPad. Consequently, I can work anywhere as long as I have Wi-Fi (thank goodness for hotspotting from my phone). I have learned to think twice before setting off for a meeting when I can get the same result without the travel time, the hassle, the expense and the associated opportunity cost.

47. GETTING TO KNOW YOUR STAFF AND THEIR WORKING DAY PREFERENCES

How well do you know the staff in your school? We may think we have developed great professional understanding, but how clued up are we about when and how they like to be contacted? For example, some people genuinely prefer out-of-hours contact, but for others, evening or weekend emails are an imposition and a source of stress.

And what about the mode of contact? Is email always the best way to get in touch? Would a quick text message be better, or is that too immediate and intrusive? And then there is the 'to Zoom or not to Zoom?' question; I like your face, but I don't need to see it every time!

To avoid any unnecessary disgruntlement in my working relationships, I always ask my colleagues about their communication preferences. I keep track of them in a one-page profile for the entire staff, detailing who likes what and when and what they don't like.

For example, by having these conversations, I discovered that one colleague always works from 6–7am every morning. She is happy to receive emails at this time, so that is when she receives emails from me. Most apps have an email scheduling facility, so don't feel you have to change your own working day preferences to match those of your colleagues. I write emails when it suits me and my colleague reads them when it suits her. Perfect.

The questions you could ask to create your own communication preference profile might include: What is your preference for the timing of a staff meeting – first thing, lunchtime or after school? If after school, is that as soon as the last child has left the building or a little later? Or even at 5pm (with a cup of tea and wearing your slippers back at home)? If we don't ask, we will never know.

Another question to ask is how long they think is the ideal length for a staff meeting. I have had answers range between 30 and 60 minutes (a productive hour). You can't please everybody all the time (the unofficial motto of the SENDCO), but you will be able to vary things to please more people more often.

Asking questions and obtaining data about your staff can be useful beyond simply time and communication preferences. Have you ever asked for their views and beliefs on all matters SEND? Have you asked them what their strengths are? And their weaknesses? What about interventions they use that work well? Or what additional support or even training they would like to receive? A questionnaire would do the trick, either a physical one or a simple online one like Google Forms or SurveyMonkey.

We can't do anything about the things we don't know we don't know (the unknown unknowns), but we can address the things we do know we don't know (the known unknowns). Deliberately and methodically seeking out a school's strengths and weaknesses in terms of both knowledge and practice means we are moving beyond mere assumptions. This is something we could all benefit from doing more of in education.

48. FINDING A TIME FOR MEETINGS THAT SUITS EVERYONE: PART I

When we are arranging meetings with parents, let's not forget that they have a routine to their day too. Whether it is a younger sibling that needs a nap, a commute to or from work, the demands of caring for other relatives, shift work or even all of the above, there can be many demands on a parent's time.

It is difficult to imagine the stresses, strains and patterns of the lives of our school families, so don't. Ask them instead. Have a conversation with parents about when would suit them best for a meeting and give them some options. You might not be able to accommodate their preference every time, but at least you are trying and they can see you trying – two important landmarks on the empathy road. For example, a meeting during the school day may be convenient for some, but for others after school is a much better fit. When we employ technology we can be more flexible, even if it is a quick meeting held over Zoom on our phone while we sit in a lay-by on the way home from work.

I am not asking for us to be martyrs about this ('My wife is away on business in Australia at the moment, so can we do a Zoom at 3am please, Mrs Bootman?'), but I am suggesting that we consider the circumstances of others more often. And the starting point is to ask, not assume.

49. FINDING A TIME FOR MEETINGS THAT SUITS EVERYONE: PART II

When I worked as a teacher, early on in my career, it was the SENDCO who organised the SEND review meetings. She would draw up a timetable of thirty-minute back-to-back slots that started at 9am on the dot and ended, equally punctually, at 3pm. These slots were handed out like golden tickets – but received like parking tickets. There was no discussion, no thought for the needs of the individuals, no flexibility in either time or place. My, how things have changed.

These days, I consider what works for each individual and I give parents options, so we can find a time that is suitable for everyone. Not only does this work at a practical level, but it also makes for better meetings too. By finding a mutually convenient time, we have set the right tone for the meeting. After all, a parent who has not only lost half a day's pay for a thirty-minute meeting, but has also incurred babysitting costs and hassle, isn't necessarily going to be in the best frame of mind.

50. KEEPING THE SEESAW BALANCED

Let's be honest: we all like consistency in our lives. After the chaos of the COVID-19 pandemic, not to mention what has been happening since, the need for a sense of predictability and calm is greater than ever for all of us, especially our children. For many children with additional needs, that consistency is needed all the more, and can be the difference between a day that goes well and one that everyone would rather forget.

Day follows night, maths follows registration, English follows lunch and all is well. But, suddenly, there is a special assembly, or a theatre group is in school, or the teacher is away on a course for the afternoon, and that much needed stability has gone out of the window. Anxiety levels are rising. This might well end badly.

For many children, life is a delicately balanced seesaw, and it doesn't take much for it to tip one way or the other. I firmly believe that, as educators, we need to be constantly aware of this seesaw, and consciously doing our best to keep it as balanced as possible through the things we say and do.

For example, we need to look out for any changes on the horizon that may impact on a child's daily routine, and ensure that these deviations from the norm are considered by those who work directly with them. This could be a change of location for teaching for the day, a visitor coming into the school, Harvest Festival at the local church, the school dog being on a visit to the vet or, yes, that theatre group coming in again.

Variety and a rich curriculum are vital for every child, but the process by which changes are implemented must be handled carefully, sensitively and empathetically. Talking to the children in advance is as important as liaising with parents. They are the experts on their child and will know about possible triggers, which we may not be aware of as educators.

I once heard of a child who presented as calm and confident in his usual classroom environment. So far, so good. A school trip was coming up, but as the child hadn't set off any alarm bells there was no pre-trip meeting with the parents. Suddenly, he found himself in a large open space and quickly turned into an insecure and anxious individual, unable to cope with the environment in which he now found himself. Staff had to act quickly to find him a quiet space in which to regain his composure and feel safer and calmer again.

It was only on return to school and a debrief with his parents that it turned out the child was never taken to large open spaces without first identifying his 'safe place' in case it all got too much. It was a seesaw incident waiting to happen, and one that could have been avoided with better awareness and communication.

51. SETTING TIMESCALES

The worst thing about writing a to-do list is the point when it turns into a things-I-failed-to-do list. Such a metamorphosis is demotivating, and it isn't a great thing to do to ourselves if we are keen to stay emotionally well. The job is challenging enough without making a record of our daily failures.

For me, setting timescales is key for two reasons. Firstly, breaking down tasks helps to compartmentalise them and make them more manageable, avoiding that sense of powerlessness, overwhelm and failure. I use a weekly planner and write down allocated times for specific tasks, which I find helps me to break up my day systematically. This, in turn, allows me to be realistic about what I can achieve each day and avoids the to-do/failed-to-do mutation. As time has gone on in my role, I have become better at gauging how much time certain tasks will take. It isn't an exact science but you do get the hang of it. The weekly planner is also a useful written record of what you have been up to, ready to show to anyone who might be interested in how you spend your week.

I also use a yearly planner to identify all the key moments across the year. This is especially important when there are meetings and events that must happen at a set time, like the school census. I need to ensure that all the information for this is collated well in advance, so it can be looked at before the big day – something I need to factor in the week before. Education, health and care plan (EHCP) reviews are another example. I like to send the paperwork out well ahead of time to ensure parents have time to read through and complete any necessary forms before the review meeting. Meetings attended by outside agencies are another example of events that go in my longer term planner, to make sure they have plenty of notice (and no excuses).

The second reason for setting timescales is so you can show your line manager what the coming week, month and year looks like. It alerts them to times when you will be particularly busy and so unavailable for other meetings, as well as quieter times (I know, it is all relative!) when you will be more available for planning and review meetings, for example – the important but not urgent parts of the job.

52. JUST SAY NO!

Once upon a time, when I was a wet-behind-the-ears teacher in a new school, a colleague asked me to 'help' relabel the reading scheme books. I was more than happy to be of assistance, so I agreed. It then transpired that the member of staff expected me to do this in my half-term holiday. What is more, by 'help' they meant 'do it all', as they weren't going to be around. Once I realised I was being asked to do something my colleague simply didn't want to do, I politely declined. Remember that saying no is as professional an act as saying yes.

As SENDCOs, we often take on tasks that, even though they are suited to our clearly amazing and expansive skill set, are just not part of our job description. I am not saying be a complete jobsworth, but doing things that aren't part of your role takes you away from the essential things that are.

It is important to know what is in your job description and what isn't. Make sure you have a copy in your filing system and check back on it if necessary. When in doubt, consult your line manager, who is the person who will be most concerned about you not doing your actual job.

Remember, questioning whether you should be doing something is a professionally positive act. It ensures that your energy is being used for the right reasons. Incidentally, there may be aspects of your role that others could do more quickly and efficiently, helping you to conserve your energy for the parts of the job where you are needed the most. For example, when I need information to be collated for an application to an outside agency, the admin team are far better suited to this task than I could ever be, and they have the data to hand without having to rifle through filing cabinets.

53. DON'T MAKE A BEELINE TO A DEADLINE

Before you set a deadline for someone else, stop and think. The workload that teachers carry is challenging enough without us adding to the pressure with a badly thought-through time limit. If we are a non-teaching SENDCO, we are definitely adding fuel to that particular fire.

If we want things to be done well, it is important that we keep to our empathy road and take into account the busy lives of the people we are asking to take on extra tasks. This is tricky to manage if you are anything like me and you want things done now or, preferably, yesterday. Before you think about setting deadlines for others, take a look at the school diary and make sure you stay away from busy periods. Data input times, report writing season, parents' evening weeks – these are all off limits.

This might take a lot of will power from you but it will pay off. It also means that when something does need to be done quickly, staff know you are only asking because it must be important. I had such an experience during lockdown. Life was already difficult for class teachers, and then here was little old me asking them for more. What was great was that they not only rose to the challenge but also helped me when my own energy levels were flagging, giving me an energy boost when I needed it most.

54. PACE YOURSELF

When travelling down the empathy road, it is important to remember that you are in a marathon, not a sprint. We SENDCOs are doers and fixers, otherwise we wouldn't be in the job. By our nature, we want to implement systems and strategies to get everything working seamlessly. We want lots of them and we want them now. So, come on, let's go! What are you waiting for, people? Follow me!

We need to understand that this approach is neither healthy nor desirable. Dorothy arriving at the Emerald City panting for breath and all alone isn't quite the outcome we want. Putting ourselves under undue and unnecessary pressure is simply setting ourselves up to fail.

I find that remembering to keep the children at the centre of everything I do helps me to pace myself better. After all, it is better to do one thing well than lots of things half-cocked. It is a good mantra to live by on a day-to-day basis.

Sometimes it is vital that you simply stop, breathe and ground yourself. Ask yourself what is most important today and what is achievable. If you are new to the role, start as you mean to go on. You might want to make your mark quickly, but there will be time for that. Get to know existing systems first and work out how you will incorporate them – or otherwise – into the SEND development plan.

55. THE SEND DEVELOPMENT PLAN

Preparing an effective development plan takes time and care. As a newly appointed SENDCO, the processes that need to be changed might appear obvious, but perhaps they exist for a good reason. I experienced this when I was new to a job and observing interventions with which I wasn't au fait. My immediate reaction was to question their validity. However, after discussing the strategies with class teachers and seeing them in action, I began to see the positive impact they were having. I ended up planning how they could be used in other settings. Getting rid of too much too soon might make matters worse today and also store up problems for the long term.

If, on the other hand, you have been in your role for a while, what needs to be changed might not be all that obvious. You may find yourself doing things the way you have always done them, which might be both wrong for today and cause all sorts of problems further down the line.

It is essential to constantly reappraise your systems and put them into one of three boxes: keep, tweak or ditch. Whether you are keen to change everything or nothing, there are always ways in which systems can be improved. By evaluating them on an ongoing basis and putting them into one of these three categories, your SEND development plan will be up to date, worthwhile and effective in the lives of your children.

56. AUDITING SEND PROVISION

Repeat after me: *An audit is not a witch-hunt.* It is important that an audit of the SEND provision in your school is a positive experience for all. If it isn't, like a massage or a fondue party, you are doing it wrong.

The overriding purpose of the audit is to address the questions, 'What are we doing well?' and 'What can we do better?' It is as simple as that. That said, it is also important to make sure that everyone involved understands that any new ideas coming out of the review process won't entail more work for anyone. You are improving, not adding.

A good starting point is to identify in advance which aspects of your SEND provision we want to audit. Where is the need? The itch to be scratched? It might be record-keeping, timetabling, monitoring, adult support in class, EHCP review systems, referral systems or something else completely.

For example, an audit of referrals might identify that too many are being rejected when they go to panel. This would then lead us to look at how we screen individuals in the first instance, before parents and staff fill in the copious amounts of paperwork needed. By addressing this, we have an opportunity to create a more robust system for screening individuals as part of our referral system.

We aren't doing the audit to point fingers; we are doing it to make improvements.

57. CENSUS AND CENSUS-ABILITY

A whirlwind of chaos is how I would describe the first time I had to complete the SEND register for the school census. I was told that the register needed to be up to date and include the right codes. What didn't help was, firstly, the deadline was the following day and, secondly, I didn't have any idea what they were talking about and wasn't convinced that 'What codes?' was going to be the best response.

What I have now, but didn't even know I needed then, is a 'living' SEND register – an ongoing, continually updated document which can be accessed at any time. In this way, when census time comes round again – as it does, once a term, like clockwork – I can signpost the document to the relevant individuals a week or so before it is due.

58. SPENDING TIME IN THE SLOW LANE

Sometimes we need to consciously move into the slow lane of the empathy road in order to take in everything that is happening around us and everything we have achieved so far. Being a SENDCO is such a busy, demanding and full-on job that, without spending at least a bit of time at a slower pace, we miss so much.

To help, I have a slow lane list. These are things that I would like to do and would enjoy doing if I had the time, such as popping into classes to see the children, finding resources to support specific individuals, or finding books and online resources that will help my colleagues. Not urgent but very rewarding.

So, every now and again, take your foot off the pedal and do the things you want to do but never seem to have time for. It will refuel you and help you to travel further in the long run.

59. MAKING TECHNOLOGY WORK FOR YOU AND SAVE TIME

I try to create a one-page profile for every child in my schools using an online document editor. It has been a game changer for me. I can send the file to parents, who complete it and then send it back to me in such a clever and timesaving way, which is nothing short of amazing.

What takes it to the next level is that parents can update the profile as they see fit. Enabling parents to participate in creating their own child's documentation has yielded many benefits in my work. Apart from helping me to stay up to date with children's needs, likes and dislikes (which can change all the time as they grow), it is now a transparent process that builds trust and collaboration between home and school.

What is more, this online profile is another 'living' document that staff can consult in order to better cater for the needs of the individual child. This is a great example of what I mean by making technology work for you and save time.

Use tech = better job + less time. I am thinking about getting some T-shirts made emblazoned with that formula!

60. TINY TECHNOLOGICAL STEPS AND THE WAY TO MAKE BIG CHANGES

Another T-shirt mantra I like the look of is 'Think small and big things happen'. Every little step I have made on my technology journey has been as a result of a specific problem that tech has been able to address. There has never been a great technological revolution where I have thrown away all my filing cabinets and replaced them with an app, and nor have I deployed the tech simply because it looked good or made me look good. I am an advocate of technology, not a missionary.

One of the benefits of this step-by-step approach is that the process has been relatively painless. I have spotted a problem, identified whatever technological response I needed to tackle that problem and then implemented it. In this way, new processes have quickly become a habitual part of my day-to-day routines.

That isn't to say that everything I have tried has been a roaring success, but at least I have established what doesn't work for me. For example, making notes on a tablet with a stylus hasn't worked for me; typing is more my thing. Dictating notes from meetings into a voice recognition app also has its limitations, although it is quite entertaining to read back.

Isolate the problem, identify the possible technological solution, give it a go and find out what suits you. If it helps you to save time and do your job more effectively, then go for it. If it doesn't hit those two important buttons, put the stylus down and step away from the tablet.

Keeping an eye out for what others are doing can be useful too. I had never heard of desktop sticky notes until I saw a colleague's screen. Mind blown! Virtual sticky notes on my desktop? Yes please. In turn, I have spread the word, so there is now an epidemic of virtual sticky notes wherever I have visited. I always chuckle as I 'recycle' my virtual sticky notes!

61. MAKING YOURSELF POPULAR THANKS TO TECH

As you can see, I am excited about how using technology can make my life easier. It also makes me (even) more popular with my colleagues, as my tech solutions mean they save time and hassle too.

Let me give you an example. When I am filling in an EHCP application, I need to collate many pieces of information from the school office, such as attendance, ethnicity, language spoken, date when the child started school and so on. Rather than bothering the office staff by bombarding them with emails or giving them lots of colour coordinated real-life sticky notes covered with questions (yes, I have tried these approaches in the past), I now make (another) live document which the office can complete and send the information back to me in their own time.

This way of working means I can keep staff in the loop about my work in general or a specific case in particular. I can also gather their views and experience without having to organise face-to-face meetings every time I need their input.

My working life has transformed from rummaging around in filing cabinets trying to find the information I need about a particular child or process to having an up-to-date document with multiple relevant authors at the touch of a button. Have a long, hard stare at the processes in your school and what technological systems already exist (e.g. SIMS, Google Classroom, a Moodle of some sort) that you could tap into. Ask your admin team if you aren't sure.

'Use tech. Make friends'. Another great T-shirt slogan.

62. PDF = PDQ

The PDF is your friend, so don't be scared of it. For example, you can use the snipping tool and simply cut and paste information from a PDF into your own document without having to tediously retype everything, especially text from a table or diagram. Perhaps this isn't news to you, but it has saved me and my colleagues a lot of time. What is more, PDFs make sharing documents – such as EHCP applications – with outside agencies much easier and more professional.

Be a tech detective like me. Ask those with whom you work about their time-saving tech ideas and keep your eyes peeled for what others are using. I find that most people have one or two hacks and shortcuts they are particularly fond of. They often assume that everyone else knows about them, but this isn't always the case. Shift + Command + 3 on a Mac for an instant screenshot, anyone?

63. THE POWER OF THE SECOND MONITOR

Thanks to having to travel between four different schools, my office has to be as portable and lightweight as possible. Above all, it has to fit into my rucksack, or 'ruffice' as I call it. Portable does not always make for ease of use, though. Scrolling up, down and between important documents and spreadsheets on a single, small screen was making life a bit stressful for me.

The solution? A portable monitor that I carry around in the ruffice which allows me to see the information I need on two different screens. You would be amazed at how this simple and not-too-expensive solution makes the whole process far easier and much less headache provoking. Definitely another game changer.

Another great innovation to find its way into my ruffice recently is a folding Bluetooth keyboard. It is about the size of a biggish mobile phone when folded up and, when unfolded and hooked up, turns my iPad into a laptop, especially when I link my iPad to my mobile phone for internet connectivity.

Again, it is all about identifying the specific problems you have and then being open and creative about how technology can help you to overcome them. Where there is a will, there is usually a technological way.

64. QUICK, SPLIT!

I could literally fill this book with tips and hacks I have learned that have helped me to save time and sweat in my SENDCO role. I will just give you one more as it was another game changer when my son first showed me.

If you are a toggler, you will know that you can move between the various windows you have open at any given time – for example, from a website to a Word or Google Docs file. You can save yourself some worry when you think you have lost a document by learning how to split your screen, so both windows are available to you at the same time. On a Windows keyboard, simply press the Windows key and the right-hand arrow and, hey presto, you have a split screen. On a Mac, hover your cursor (hark at me, the tech guru!) over the green button in the top left of any application (which you have never noticed until just this second). Hover, I said, don't click! Three options pop up – full screen, tile window to left and tile window to right – and you just choose the one you want. You are welcome.

65. KEEPING YOUR EHCPS UP TO DATE

We maintain our EHCPs as 'living' Word documents and annotate them throughout the year. This keeps all the information current and means that when we have an annual review we have all the data to hand, instead of having a lengthy meeting to collate what we need. It also shows progress over the year and is a great document to share with parents. I can type up notes on the EHCP during a meeting, which is also a great timesaver. In this way, the EHCP is a document we refer to frequently, keeping it live and at the forefront of everyone's minds throughout the school year.

As we saw in tip 62, sometimes you will need to share documents like EHCPs as a PDF (which can't be edited by the receiver). Make sure you know how to save a Word document as a PDF (hint – one way is via File and Save As) and also how to turn a PDF into a Word document (File and Convert To Word). Depending on the package you use, this can be as simple as clicking on the document and then opening it in Word. Again, small things making a big difference to busy lives.

66. A VIRTUAL SEND RESOURCE LIBRARY, ANYONE?

For the last year, I have been collating all the SEND resources I can find and putting them online for staff to access. It has taken a while, but, boy, has it been worth it. It has made it so much easier to signpost material to staff, it is already saving me time further down the line, and it is making me look switched on and professional (if I say so myself).

The virtual SEND resource library is a real timesaver for SENDCOs. For example, staff can now access the resources themselves, from home if they like, rather than having to find them at school. It also makes it easier to pool resources, as one person doesn't have to rely on someone else to bring something into school.

I am also in the process of adding a list to the library of the best SEND books we have in school, including my own personal favourites. I post a picture of the book along with the back-cover blurb to whet people's appetites. In addition, I can keep virtual tabs on who has what and when, as books have a tendency to wander off if we aren't careful.

67. PAPER-FREE FREEDOM

It was a big step. I knew that we all wanted to save time and technology was probably the answer, but paperless? Foregoing the pen and the paper so beloved by the teaching profession – was I mad?

At this point, I was a SENDCO across two primary schools. I was convinced that paperless was the way to go, even if I didn't know how to set about it at first. However, I knew enough about technology, people and people-and-technology to know I needed to start small. Little steps were what was needed. Nothing too scary, at least to begin with.

My first step was thinking through the process of turning my dog-eared, sticky note-stuffed, highlighter pen-filled paper diary into something that would work online for everyone, especially me. Now, I know that choosing next year's academic diary is one of the highlights of the stationery year for many teachers – a harbinger of summer, like seeing the first swallow or thinking life will be easier after the SATs have finished. Then, there are all the decisions – spiral bound or stitched binding? Elastic band or magnetic clip to keep it shut? Monogram initials on the cover, or is that a bit up yourself? So many choices. But the modern world is waiting, and paper doesn't grow on trees, so I made the decision to take my time planning online.

I found out what people were already using within my schools and replicated the same system. For us it was Google Calendar. It is important to use a system that is established across the school, so it is easy to sync your diaries. This worked well for sharing with staff when I was free to attend meetings, and when I started adding my personal commitments to the online calendar, they knew when and when not to book time with me.

Seeing how well this move online was received, and how useful it was to my job, I decided to take things to the next level. Firstly, though, it was necessary to make a pact with myself. I determined to go paperless from a set date and to move forward, not backwards. The last thing I was going to do was go back through the files and make the past paperless too. Life was too short to spend hours digitising the content of a row of filing cabinets, unless the document was specifically needed for something important like an EHCP – and, even then, only if I was sure it was really necessary.

68. JUST ONE LOOK AND THEN MY HEART WENT BOOM

March 2020. How can we forget? An event that had started on the other side of the world and we had only caught sight of out of the corner of our eye suddenly hit us slap-bang in the face. Everything changed overnight.

When the pandemic struck, I know I wasn't alone in responding with 'not in a month of Sundays' to the request to teach online during lockdown. I am a people person, and it is all about the face to face. I became acutely aware that, when it came to technology, I had been involved in some sort of weird bartering system in which I would trade the wiping of noses, a Year 1 assembly or dealing with a difficult parent in return for technological favours. Now, my bartering buddies were isolating, as was I. Like everyone else, I was on my own.

As the realisation dawned that I was going to have to shift from thinking about teaching online to actually doing it, I understood what my biggest fear was – and I bet it was the same for you. It was doing it wrong and looking foolish. The same as in the real world, to be honest, so perfectly get-overable as long as you put children at the heart of your work.

Everyone has glitches when they move online. 'Your mic isn't on' became the catchphrase of 2020. I persevered and practised. I moved around the house and had video conference meetings with my husband to make sure I knew how it all worked. I even thought about hitting the 'Breakout' button to see what would happen.

When the time came for my first online lesson, it wasn't without trepidation that I hit 'Launch meeting' on Zoom and found myself face to virtual face with a group of anxious but bemused-looking reception children and their favourite teddies, as requested. Following my personal fast-food restaurant mantra of 'Go big or go home', I decided that we would start with a virtual Hokey Cokey, something that doesn't suffer an online time delay lightly. Next up in my lesson (and I do use the term lightly in this instance) was an impromptu wooden spoon and plastic bowl percussion experience which would have made the Cadbury's gorilla weep. The fact that we were joined in our Tupperware symphony by so many parents, as anxious and bemused as their children, meant that all my online inhibitions and misgivings were soon cast aside.

After this intrepid start, I felt as if I could take on the world. Now, with that first lockdown becoming a distant memory, my life is full of virtual meetings and I thoroughly embrace the hybrid nature of my job. The lesson from all of this? Face your fears, lose your blinkers and sometimes it doesn't matter if your left arm is going in when someone else's is going out. That is what it is all about, after all.

69. SPREAD THE LOAD WITH A SPREADSHEET

Some people go all gooey-eyed at the thought of creating a spreadsheet. They love its meticulous predictability and the way in which all the chaos in the universe can be tamed into little boxes with a formula attached. I was petrified; it was like maths but disguised.

The turning point came when someone sat me down and showed me in a really simple manner how to use a spreadsheet. Yes, it can do all sorts of things but, like a Swiss Army knife, you will never use most of them (even some Swiss soldiers don't know what all the tools are for).

Once I had been shown in such a straightforward way, my fear fell away. I also learned that if I got stuck on anything, I just needed to search on YouTube and there would be a video explaining what to do – a video I could pause and rewind as I sorted out myself and my spreadsheet. Now, everything made sense and yesterday's complex had become today's simple.

I now use spreadsheets on a daily basis, not quite gooey-eyed but not wild-eyed with fear either – for example, my to-do list and daily timetable are spreadsheets. I am still no expert, but I made sure I overcame my trepidation as I knew it would help me to help the children better. I found someone to support me and learned in little steps and at my own pace. This approach should be at the heart of your own technological revolution.

70. GIVING CHILDREN WHO ARE NEW TO OUR SETTINGS THE BEST START POSSIBLE

Being flexible is always vital when working with children with additional needs. This is all the more so when it comes to starting a new school. Letting go of old routines can be as unsettling as having to learn new ones, and the beginning and end of the day can be a real point of anxiety and stress.

Fortunately, there are some great minds at work offering practical ideas and suggestions. When it comes to the beginning of the school day, it can be a bit frenetic and disturbing for the best of us, let alone a child who is anxious. Allowing the child to come in just a few minutes after the mad rush can make a big difference to how well their day starts and, by extension, how their day plays out.

On the flip side of this flexibility is consistency. For some children, it is the need to know what is happening and when that can make all the difference. In some cases, when a child is starting school by spending small but increasing amounts of time in class, it can be beneficial to keep the end time the same. They come in at 2.30pm and leave at 3pm. Then they come in at 2pm but still leave at 3pm. Regularity and consistency are built in from the outset, which are both vital for our children.

Flexibility, empathy and talking to parents will help you to identify any issues in advance and come up with creative ways to address them. Often, they are just little things but can make a huge difference in the lives of the family.

71. LUNCHTIMES AS A TRIGGER FOR CHILDREN WITH ADDITIONAL NEEDS

Another potentially stressful time for children just starting school is lunchtime. Routines, noise, smells, so many children and adults, scary dinner ladies. It is a lot to take in.

One system I have seen working to great effect is for children who find lunchtime overwhelming to sit at a table in a corridor rather than in the lunch hall itself. Not only is it significantly quieter but they can also sit with at least some of their friends. Another variation is to seat individuals who find the experience difficult in the dining hall but at a table away from the madding crowd. They have just enough space to ease their anxieties, but they are also experiencing school life and learning to be part of it.

I have also seen new children introduced to the lunch hall experience by going in and having something to drink with their friends and then setting off for home afterwards. This systematic desensitisation approach not only gets them used to lunchtimes in a safe and considered way, but it also ensures that the last experience of the day is a positive and enjoyable one, not breathless and stressful. I will drink to that.

72. PROVIDING CHILDREN WITH THE TIME AND SPACE THEY NEED

You know how it works by now. The child experiences what is perceived as a threat. The stress hormone cortisol kicks into action, doing what it is there to do – protect the child. One or more of the fight, flight, freeze, flock or faint responses are activated. And suddenly you have a classroom or playground situation on your hands.

This physiological response can result in the child become threatening and perhaps verbally or even physically aggressive. In such an emotionally hijacked state, apart from making sure everyone is safe, your only real ally here is time. In my experience, when this happens, children need to be given space and time to regulate themselves. Dr Andrew Curran writes about this brilliantly in his book *The Little Book of Big Stuff About the Brain*: 'the first step is to calm them down sufficiently so that their amygdalas aren't short-circuiting out their higher brain'. He adds that this can be seen in 'underlying behavioural strategies such as "Stop" or "Time out" where a child is given time in their own space to calm down.'[5] I have seen this work really well in many settings.

The key here is to help the child learn to self-regulate. There are many individuals with expertise in this area, including Dr Pooky Knightsmith (@PookyH, www.pookyknightsmith.com). Make sure everyone knows the routine when this is necessary and that there is an area within the classroom where the children can go to regain their calm and composure as they self-regulate. Such areas might

---

5   A. Curran, *The Little Book of Big Stuff About the Brain* (Independent Thinking Series) (Carmarthen: Crown House Publishing, 2008), pp. 157, 160.

have a blackout tent or sensory toys and soothing music playing. Again, speak to parents and the child about what helps when the inevitable happens.

73. PUTTING OURSELVES IN THE SHOES OF THE CHILDREN WE TEACH: PART I

It is true what they say: walking a mile in someone else's shoes takes you a long way down the empathy road. For example, take the situation where a child has done something they now regret. Apart from the fact that a child who has been severely triggered may well not remember how they responded, such is the extent of the brain hijack, is making the child relive the experience the best way forward? Would you like that for yourself?

For me, this where the PACE approach (described in tip 4) really comes into its own. To recap, it is the brainchild of clinical psychologist Dan Hughes, who has worked with Kim Golding and colleagues to really bring this approach to life. PACE provides a way of working with children and their behaviour in a reflective, positive and constructive way.

74. PUTTING OURSELVES IN THE SHOES OF THE CHILDREN WE TEACH: PART II

Picture the scene. One child has hit another in the face with a ball during a PE lesson. Now what?

By applying the PACE approach when I found myself in this situation, it was amazing what played out. My first act was to call over the boy who had thrown the ball. Despite deliberately not using my angry Mrs Bootman voice, his immediate response was a defensive (and not entirely unreasonable), 'Go on, shout at me like everyone else does. I won't listen anyway.' By not shouting, but remaining playful (but firm) and curious, we ascertained that he didn't mean to do it, that he was sorry and that he would do his best not to do it again. It was a PE lesson, after all, and collateral damage can occur.

What was even more insightful – and worrying – was that this child wanted to be shouted at. By playing his part in that game, the teacher's angry comments would have passed over his head. He had learned not to listen. What he told me in that brief exchange was a sign that more conversations were needed. Over the coming weeks, I was able to understand him far more as an individual, and not just the 'you need to keep an eye on that one' boy. We started to build connections, and connections lead to belonging, and belonging matters. For example, I discovered that he enjoyed walking with his family, which in turn led to more chats about his likes and dislikes and his family life.

The PACE approach has helped me to initiate conversations that have built connections with many children over the years, forming what I think of as a spider's web of trust around and between the whole school community.

75. WHEN DIFFICULT CONVERSATIONS WITH CHILDREN SURPRISE

When you have invested a great deal of time and effort in building a relationship with a child, and then it falls to you to have that difficult conversation because of their unacceptable actions, it is hard. Our instinct is to worry that all the time we have spent connecting and building trust will evaporate when we point out what they have done wrong and set in motion a suitable sanction. But children can and will surprise you. That relationship you have taken so much care to nurture – the web you have spun around the child – might mean more to them than you suspected.

It was as a result of just such a situation that I found myself sitting on the floor of a school corridor, side by side with a child whose behaviour had fallen well outside of what was acceptable. Sitting alongside, not face to face, is a powerful way to have a balanced and reflective conversation. Looking back, I feel that the environment – somewhere neutral, non-intimidating and unexpected – played an important part in what transpired.

Before I could begin the conversation, the child burst out with, 'Mrs Bootman, I know I've done something I shouldn't have. I'll try not to do it again, I honestly will, but I don't think I've earned the right to stay for the after-school film. We need to ring my mum so I can go home at the end of the day.' My jaw dropped and my heart felt full. This child had not only taken ownership of what he had done, but he had also identified a sanction that he felt was suitable. He did indeed go home at the end of the day, but not before I had told his parents not only what misdemeanour he had committed but how he had also owned his actions.

A conversation I was dreading had become a moment of pride. The event didn't break the connection and trust we had built up over time but strengthened it.

76. THE IMPORTANCE OF LIAISING WITH PRESCHOOLS AND PREVIOUS SCHOOLS

There is always a lot of paperwork involved in helping a child to either join or leave your school, but paperwork is never enough. It only tells half the story, and our most vulnerable children need their full story to be told.

The face-to-face conversations that SENDCOs and teachers have about the child, about where they have come from and where they are going next, are so important. It is here that you can explore the true essence of the child, the day-to-day support they require and the strategies that are working well at the moment, beyond what is on their EHCP or other official documents. Besides, this paperwork can get out of date quickly and can end up giving the wrong impression of a child and their needs.

These conversations, done well, will ensure the child feels at home the minute they walk through the door. Remember to keep these lines of communication open after the transition or transfer too. You never know when they will come in handy.

77. MAKE THE PERSON BEHIND THE COUNTER AT THE POUND SHOP YOUR BEST FRIEND

Plastic fishbowls. You know you want them. No? Well, that is because you simply haven't yet understood their true potential.

I have been a fan of the pound shops for many years, spotting items and thinking, 'How could I use that in my school?' I know I am not alone. My view is that there are two sorts of teachers – those who are pound shop fans and those who aren't yet pound shop fans.

A few years ago, I was doing my usual pound shop visit when I saw them. Plastic goldfish bowls. Twenty of them. A box full. I knew I had struck plastic gold. My mind immediately wandered to the old-fashioned cupboard I had in my classroom at that time, with its beautiful wooden shelves behind a well-worn door. Perfect.

I had the door taken off the cupboard and, using the goldfish bowls, I created the most amazing pick 'n' mix of colourful and enticing stationery, toys, puzzles and more. Want some Lego? Check out the goldfish bowl on the cupboard shelves. Need a fidget toy? Third goldfish bowl from the right, second shelf down. Did someone say pompoms? Over there – and put them back when you are done. It was the most wonderful addition to my classroom and didn't break the bank.

What was special was that the children could help themselves. They didn't need my permission. From a special needs point of view, a child who might have difficulty reading the word 'Scissors' on a tin, box or drawer could now collect the scissors from the goldfish bowl without fuss or embarrassment or the intervention of an adult.

It is another example, one of many I hope in this book, of little things making a massive difference.

78. THINK BEFORE YOU SPEND!

When you are considering resources for a child with additional needs, first think outside the (money) box. For example, if a child needs to do exercises in order to improve their gross motor skills, such as pushing, pulling and resistance, why not give them a PE mat turned upside down (so there is low friction) and get them to pull the mat along the hall? I have also purchased a variety of different strength (and cheap) resistance bands, and the children choose which one they want on a particular day. The element of choice is one of the reasons it works so well.

Children also love the idea of selecting items for their sensory box. The 'sweet shop' they choose from consists of an array of different items of varying textures and sizes (and, in the case of resistance bands, give), such as feathers, sand, bubble wrap, pom-poms or dried beans/lentils. Each child can pick what they would like on a specific day and place it in their own lidded box, which has their name on it so that it is personal to them.

These items can give children comfort and help them to self-regulate: the tickle of feathers on skin, the grittiness of sand, the satisfying popping of bubble wrap, the softness of pom-poms and the sifting and scooping of dried pulses. However, what can be soothing for one individual can be dysregulating for another, which is why it is important to give children ownership of their own sensory box. Little choices like this add up to a crucial sense of agency and belonging, which children need to thrive in our classrooms. The day I let the children choose the items they wanted to put in their sensory box was a real turning point for me. It was when I realised that I didn't know what was best for them; they did.

Choosing is a factor at play in another activity that brings huge benefits at no extra cost. It is an activity I use whenever I think the children need a sensory break, while also helping them to think about weights and measures. My children love carrying around those large bottles of paint, the ones with the handles. They get to select a bottle to take for a walk down the corridor and back again for a quick learning break. It is great to see them working out before they go how heavy or light the bottle will be, depending on how much paint is left in it. They sometimes involve me too, and we have an in-depth discussion about which one they would prefer to carry at that moment. Once again, they are making a choice, learning to live with the consequences (those full paint pots can get heavy for little hands by the time they get to the end of the corridor and are ready to turn around) and they are enjoying a sense of ownership.

Sometimes it is the children's fine motor skills that need to be developed, which is when I dig out the Tupperware again (once the Zoom drum band have finished with it) and fill the boxes with salt or other little grains. I then find some small items, which I know will be of interest to the child, such as Lego figures, buttons, corks or beads (if you play detective you will soon find out their likes), which I hide in the salt. And then, with the addition of a cheap pair of tweezers, voilà, an instant game of digging for treasure that exercises the children's focus, concentration and those all-important motor skills. They love this game, I assure you.

Another activity that involves simply repurposing equipment the school already has is to assemble a raiding party and head to the PE cupboard. Once there, gather up kits like those little rubber quoits, balls of varying sizes, skittles and hoops. Once back in the classroom, we design a short course together, including activities like bouncing a ball or jumping in and out of a hoop for a set number of times. I use chalk to mark on the wall how many times I want them to do each exercise, although sometimes the children throw a dice to decide the number. Once they have completed the activity for the required number of times, they move on to the next item on the course.

Sensory breaks and healthy activities that grow mind and body, not to mention that sense of choice and control – and fun too! All of these activities involve very little or no expense. This not only makes them easy to implement in the classroom, but also, if they prove to be not quite right for your children, you haven't wasted too much of the school (or family) budget.

79. MY FAVOURITE THINGS

I am not sure about whiskers on kittens and warm woollen mittens, but plastic pegs and milk bottle tops are definitely up there. I think I could write a book about things to do with plastic pegs!

One simple game is to get the children to attach pegs to coat hangers to develop their fine motor skills. Another activity involves drawing a line down the middle of the table. On my side, I create patterns out of pegs – they might be separate or pegged together – and the children have to recreate the patterns on their side of the table. They love it.

Peg power fades to insignificance when it comes to the fun to be had with plastic milk bottle tops. To begin with, a colleague put out a plea to parents to ask them to collect the red, green and blue tops, depending on what kind of milk they drank in their household (no judgements were made, honest). We soon ended up with enough bottle tops to start our own dairy, so now the possibilities were endless.

A great starting point for taking the lid off fun with bottle tops is to let the children make up games themselves. Their creativity is absolutely endless. It might be that they find ways to recreate their own versions of noughts and crosses, Othello or Connect 4, or it might be that they come up with some new games.

A bucket full of milk bottle tops can give playful and curi-ous SENDCOs and teachers amazing insights into the working of children's brains too. On one occasion, I was going to play a game using milk bottle tops with two chil-dren. Initially, we all had to pick the colour we wanted. I chose blue and one of the children chose green. Of course, going last is no choice at all, but rather than settling for red the remaining child chose green. Now what? As the adult in the room, the way I saw it was that I was faced with three choices: (a) ask child number 3 to choose another colour, effectively to take red; (b) ask child number 1 to take red, possibly with a bit of bribery thrown in; or (c) channel my inner King Solomon and quickly come up with the idea that they could both be green, but one places their bottle tops face up and the other face down. I was quite pleased with myself for that one! What I hadn't factored in was (d): the second child changes his mind, goes for red and says, 'Can we start now, Miss …?'

80. GINNY THE WALKING PINTEREST BOARD

The next time you are in your kitchen waiting for the kettle to boil and wondering what you have done with your life, have a quick look round for things you aren't using at home but that would be great in school. No, not the Russell Hobbs food processor you bought in a post-*Bake Off* final haze a few years ago. I mean the little things. Look in your kitchen drawers, for example. If you are anything like me you will spot small scoops, Tupperware boxes without lids and lids without boxes, tweezers, tongs, an old golf ball (not that anyone in your family plays golf), something a dog chewed (and you don't have a dog either), unused plastic cutlery, disposable paper cups and plates, an excessive number of sieves, the object you don't recognise but don't want to throw out. There is lots of stuff that will transmute from clutter to gold the minute it arrives in school. The list is endless. We just need to open our minds to what we can achieve with the things we stockpile.

In my experience, children love to use tweezers to move 'treasure' from one Tupperware box to another. It is an excellent way to focus their concentration and develop fine motor skills. They also like to group objects by size or colour. You could also play observation and memorisation games, like Kim's Game, which was always a favourite at birthday parties long ago. Place a number of items on a tray (things they can remember easily like a pencil, paperclip, wooden spoon, peg) and cover them with a cloth.

Have a big unveil and invite the children to memorise the contents of the tray. Re-cover them and ask the children to list the items, or return the tray with one item removed and get them to identify the missing object.

I was once described by a teaching assistant as a 'walking Pinterest board'. I will own that, and I advocate that you all open your kitchen drawers and become walking Pinterest boards along with me.

81. THE FLEXIBLE CLASSROOM

As teachers, we all have our own teaching styles along with tried and tested ways in which we like to set up our class-room. In my privileged and peripatetic position as a SENDCO across four schools, and with experience in many others, it is obvious that classroom approaches and lay-outs that one colleague regards as good practice, others will find difficult to understand, maddening or even downright unprofessional. Nowhere is this more apparent than in the thorny question about where children sit.

This is a contentious subject, but one that needs further discussion when it comes to supporting children with additional needs in a caring and empathetic way. I have always been more than happy to allow children to sit where they wanted at the beginning of the school year, the only caveat being that they do their best wherever they choose to sit. This has worked pretty well most of the time. However, I have known teachers move into full-on wedding planning mode, spending ages working out who will sit where by moving sticky notes around on a diagram of their classroom or devising an intricate spreadsheet seating plan.

Where do you sit on an INSET day or when you go on a course – with a friend, with a complete stranger or, worse still, with people you don't really like because 'it will do you good'? Or, dare I raise it, are you told where to sit? I believe that children need to feel happy about where they sit, as long as our expectations about behaviour and achievement are high and explicit. We can do children a disservice by deciding on their behalf who is the best person for them to sit next to. As I have said before, do unto others as you would have them do unto you.

What isn't next to them is important too. How much space do they have around their seat? It was fascinating listening to my children during lockdown when we could have no more than fifteen in the classroom. They revealed how much they liked having ownership of their own desk rather than a shared space. It made me realise how much I would hate to share my desk with someone else.

Linked to this empathetic approach to personal space is to consider whether a child is right-handed or left-handed and allow sufficient space at the correct side of the desk. Also, think about where on a table they might want to position their exercise book or paper and pen. If you were to get a notebook now (or perhaps you have one with you already), where would you put it on a table in front of you in relation to this book – north, south, east or west?

All these little preferences add up to making us feel comfortable and in control of our learning space. They are really important and yet easily overlooked in a one-size-fits-all classroom environment. By having a more flexible approach to classroom layout, we can be more accommodating in allowing children to choose the set-up that best suits them. For example, different children prefer different kinds of seating. Some children may favour sitting on a special wobble cushion. Some children, whatever they are sitting on, prefer being at the front of the class. Some would rather be at the back near an edge, and some near a window. For others, that would prove too distracting and they will opt to be as far away from the window as possible.

Once again, we are talking about choice, ownership and control – that is, helping children who may feel they are lacking in ability and opportunity to make choices about their own lives and to have agency. If we don't give it to them in a caring and professional way, they end up taking it for themselves anyway. Go on, play classroom detective. Observe a class and look for clues about how the children work best, and then consider changing your classroom accordingly.

82. EVERYONE FREEZE! WE HAVE LOST DAVE!

Try this: go into an unfamiliar classroom and say to a child, 'Excuse me, can you tell me where the scissors are, please?' If you are anything like me, you will find the responses intriguing and insightful in equal measure.

In my experience, for every 'Yes, Miss, they're over there in the tin marked "Scissors". There's a picture of a pair of scissors on the tin too. Why are you asking? Do you need anything cutting? Have you lost your own? Who are you anyway?' you will receive a fair few bemused looks followed by a whole-class debate about where Miss or Sir keeps the scissors at the moment.

I find it fascinating that so many children who inhabit our classrooms don't know where these day-to-day fundamentals of school life are to be found. Surely, this makes life more difficult for everyone.

The whole subject of what goes where and how it is organised is a minefield when we are working with children with additional needs. I have seen classroom resources managed in many different ways: the children bring their own pencil cases; the school provides pencil cases; no one has a pencil case; the pens are numbered and each child is allocated a number; the glue sticks have got eyes and a mouth and each child is assigned their own named stick (hello Dave!). I have also seen whole classes having to stay in at break time because a glue stick lid has gone missing, and the child who was supposed to be using it is in tears because they have been blamed.

These systems might seem logical to a class teacher; however, for some children they actually cause lots of angst and upset. We need to consider how our systems might impact on the children in our care. More importantly, if a system isn't working for those in our care, we need to look at changing it.

83. TO TRAY OR NOT TO TRAY?

I am just going to put this out there: do you need trays in your classrooms?

When I was a class teacher, we were a no-tray classroom and everyone lived. If you do have trays in your classroom, I would like to pose this question to you: would you want to be the child whose tray is right at the bottom, the child scrabbling on your hands and knees to get your maths book while four classmates whose trays are above yours are getting theirs? Meanwhile, the teacher is telling everyone to hurry up. Stressful or what?!

If you must tray, have a think about how you organise them. Could you space them out around the room, so they are all at a sensible and accessible height for the children? What about the children who might benefit from having theirs on the desk next to them? Even better, ask the children what they would prefer. I remember one child coming up with a brilliantly well-thought-out tray system. He had scoured the classroom for suitable receptacles – one for pencils, one for his pencil sharpener and rubber and a small box with drawers (I don't know where he found that) for paperclips. It was a stationery wonder. The most important thing was that he had ownership of it and looked after it as if it were the Crown Jewels. It was amazing and something I would never have come up with.

84. THE PILLOWCASE ORGANISER

On my school detective trip to Finland (see tip 89), I saw an ingenious way of organising children's items, such as pens, pencils, reading book and so on. When not in use, all these items were stored in a 'pocket' built into the backs of their chairs. How neat! Thinking it through with my colleagues, we realised that we could recreate the same set-up using pillowcases. This involved sliding a pillowcase over the back of the chair and folding it back on itself to make a pocket. The children could then place their items into the pocket organiser and, hey presto, a clutter-free desk but with everything needed close to hand. The children loved them, and even more so when we let them personalise them too. And not a tray in sight.

85. ARE YOU THE LEGO BUILDER OR THE GETTER OF PIECES?

When building a Lego model as a pair, are you the builder or are you the one who goes off in search of the pieces? I am naturally a getter, so it makes sense for me to team up with a builder to get the job done. Neither is more important than the other; both are vital.

When you are planning teamwork exercises in the classroom, make sure that everyone's strengths and weaknesses are taken into account. This is all the more important for children with additional needs who can sometimes be overlooked or rejected in a group work setting. Make sure the SENDCO is involved in conversations about how best to organise teams and ensure the whole class knows that everyone needs to be included and valued for the unique contribution they bring to a team.

86. WOULD YOU RATHER ...?

Right answers have a lot to answer for. If all classroom life is about is the constant search for the correct answer – the one in the back of the book or in the teacher's head – then we are setting up many children not only to fail but to have a pretty miserable time in the process too.

In my work, I see children thrive when their school life is full of non-threatening experiences and interactions. Of course, there is a place for learning facts, but the more children have the opportunity to talk openly, without fear of getting it wrong, the more we see them grow and develop the confidence to learn. What is more, by giving children the opportunity to be themselves, our classrooms become places where diversity and different ways of being and thinking are permitted and celebrated. One size will never fit all because all are not one size.

A simple little game that I used to play with my class which became a highly prized morning ritual is a case in point. Perhaps you know it. The 'Would you rather …?' game involves picking two random items from whatever is around you, let's say a mug or a pen, and asking, 'Would you rather be a mug or a pen?' I remember one particularly heated discussion about whether a class would rather be Velcro or a lace on a shoe, which boiled down to not wanting to be a 'wet lace'!

It always amazed me how well this game worked, how creative the children were as they made – and defended – their choices and how it helped me to develop positive, open relationships with all the children in the class. I still use it as a way of building instant rapport when I am meeting children for the first time, helping them to overcome their anxieties and their fear of being wrong.

87. THE POWER OF TEA TO MAKE POSITIVI-TEA

If anyone comes to my house, my first thought is always to offer them a cuppa. It would be rude not to. I decided a long time ago that what is good enough for me at home is good enough for me at work, so I always offer anyone who comes to meet me at school a cup of tea.

Something as simple as offering someone a drink – whether that is a parent, colleague or someone from an outside agency – immediately makes me seem human and makes them feel welcome. Think of it like a hug in a mug.

In Denmark, they have the word 'hygge', which translates as a feeling of cosiness and conviviality. I should think the words 'hug' and 'hygge' are related somewhere down the line. With a warm brew in your hands, your meeting has already got off to a good start, with everyone calm and connected. Of course, sometimes people don't want to begin a meeting in that way. They start off wanting to be angry, to be heard, to get their point across. On these occasions, they may refuse my offer. If anyone ever does turn down a cuppa, I simply say, 'Are you sure? I'm having one.' Invariably, they change their mind, and the connection is back on track.

A mid-meeting cuppa is also useful. It provides a few minutes' break and an opportunity to have a think about what has been happening before you get going again (not to mention a quick nip to the loo).

88. WHERE TO HAVE THE MEETING

I mentioned in tip 25 that the geography of a meeting can really make or break the success of the gathering, but if the aim of the meeting is to build and not break connections, there are other factors to consider too.

Layout is one aspect. School is, and always has been, a hierarchical place. Next time you are in a school reception trying to get a smile from the receptionist, have a look at the staff photo board. How often is the head teacher at the top followed by the leadership team, the teaching staff and the teaching assistants, with the ancillary staff at the bottom, un-ironically holding up the rest of their colleagues? Think about this structure from a socio-economic point of view too: who earns the most? Who has the highest level of education?

For parents who were all too aware of the pecking order when they were at school – and where they stood in it – they may be approaching a meeting either ready to accept they are not as good as the rest or prepared to fight their corner all the more noisily because of this hierarchy.

With all of that in mind, how are you going to set out the tables and chairs for a meeting in which you want to build and cement relationships? One thing I always attempt to do is to keep the seating at the same level for everyone. Without even realising what we are doing, we can find ourselves seated in the office chair – the power chair – with the parents on lower chairs or, even worse, children's classroom chairs. If you want your meeting to have at least some chance of building positive connections, make sure you are all, literally, eye to eye.

Who sits where is an important consideration too. If all the school staff are on one side of the meeting, it can appear threatening and give off an 'us and them' vibe, which isn't (hopefully) what you are looking for. Make sure you mix things up, so the message is one of all being in it together.

Something else to think about as you hold your meeting in a picnic spot by the side of the empathy road is your body language because how we sit can give off different signals. For example, by nature, I tend to sit with my arms crossed, but I have realised that this may appear rather defensive. As a result, I now consciously sit with my arms unfolded. This may seem like a small thing but, as ever, little things can make the biggest difference. I also ensure that there is no table between me and parents in meetings. No physical barriers. Nothing that can come between us when working together for the good of the children.

89. FINNISH AS I MEAN TO GO ON

A few years ago, I was fortunate enough to go on a week-long trip to Finland to observe their education system. It is a trip that changed my outlook on so many aspects of educational life, and the lessons I learned have stayed with me. So much has been written about the Finnish system, but let me give you four examples from my experience to help you think about what we can learn for our own practice.

Firstly, I was watching a group of 3-year-olds playing outside in the sub-zero conditions. As I looked on (well wrapped up), I saw one child hit another with a shovel full of snow. Although I was ready to intervene, in my best (woolly) teacher hat, I thought it best to wait for the Finnish staff member to take action, but none was forthcoming. Later, somewhere warmer, I asked our hosts about the incident and why they didn't step in. They replied in a matter-of-fact way that if they were to deal with such altercations, then the children involved would never learn how to deal with it themselves. Such sobering words.

This led me to wonder how often we get in the way of children learning the all-important life skills they need. As SENDCOs, we are naturally compassionate (I hope) and want to help put things right. But what if that short-term fixing of issues is actually disempowering for children in the long run? Are we putting into practice the sort of tough love our children will need to develop resilience and real-world strategies to deal with people and events?

The second experience occurred as I was leaving school that day with these questions swirling round in my head. I noticed there were no fences surrounding the school. Security fences and gates are put up around primary schools in the UK to keep unwanted visitors out and the children in. Here, in Finland, the children could wander off if they wanted to, but they chose to stay because it was more interesting and safe to do so. If the children in your care could walk out of their own accord, how many would, and why? What could you do to encourage them to stay?

Classroom management and pedagogy was the third area that struck me. Lack of differentiation is a no-no in our schools, yet I saw little teacher planned extension material in Finland. When the children finished a task, they were self-motivated enough to pursue a new activity of their own choice. How can we set things up in our own classrooms so that when a child has completed a task, they can move on to something else without waiting for the teacher's input or permission? How can we ensure that, at least some of the time, the tasks children get to work on are motivating in their own right and they are doing them because they want to, not because they are expected to?

The fourth experience which really made me consider my practice and had me twitching was classroom discipline, or the lack of it. I saw children engaged in what we would consider to be low-level disruption: one child was opening and closing his desk top lid as the teacher taught and another was ceaselessly fidgeting with a piece of adhesive putty between his finger and thumb. Thinking all wasn't well in this supposed Garden of Educational Eden, my pre-conceptions about what attentive behaviour looked like were in for a shake-up when the teacher asked the class a question to check for learning and understanding. Who were the two who were first to reply, and to reply well? *Sinä arvasit sen!* It was Desk Top Lid Boy and Adhesive Putty Boy. This made me revisit my view on what environment children need in order to thrive at school.

Are our classroom expectations geared more towards what we need as teachers rather than what children need as learners? Is the policing of their behaviour (sit down, sit still, don't talk, don't fidget) counterproductive in the long run? If there was more variety in the way we taught, would there be less need for such behavioural policing? Can we create conducive classroom environments without this level of coercion, especially for our more vulnerable children? Do the children who are having trouble fitting in have something to tell us about the environment they are struggling to fit into?

These are important and controversial questions, but ones that have altered my practice since my visit – and, I believe, altered it for the better. The trip encouraged me to challenge my preconceptions about what good practice in teaching and learning looks like and to think more deeply about what the children need both now and as they mature. These were some of my first few steps along the empathy road.

90. THE PATCHWORK QUILT OF CARE

There are many people involved in the care and support given to a child with additional needs, so it is vital that we all work together. I think of this as us professionals working in harmony to create 'the patchwork quilt of care'. As with any quilt, all the individual parts need to come together and stay together, and each is as important as the next. This means that everyone's individual input is valued and listened to, but is also seen as a part of the bigger picture – the whole quilt.

This can be difficult when there are differences of opinion or suggestions and challenges that we hadn't even considered. However, exploring these differences can help us to establish the best course of action for a particular child, while thinking in terms of a patchwork quilt can ensure that we don't lose sight of the care and support we are coming together to provide for the child.

Take a recent example. We had invited an outside agent to join our team to help with a particular child whose behaviour was challenging, to say the least. This professional saw things through a different lens, not a school-based one, and it was with this distinct perspective that they were able to offer various ideas, suggestions and practices we hadn't thought of previously. By bringing in a new 'patch', but not losing sight of the bigger picture, our patchwork quilt expanded to successfully meet the needs of the child and formed a better blanket of care.

91. IS THIS MY ROLE?

SENDCOs are, by our nature, caring individuals, but our professional strength can also be a weakness if sniffed out by busy colleagues. Beware the conversation that starts with, 'You know how good you are with people ...?' because what is coming is a request to have a difficult conversation with a parent. 'You know how creative you are ...?' is a pre-cursor to someone asking you to plan a lesson they don't want to deliver. And we all know where the conversation is going that begins, 'You know how good you are at filling in forms ...?' Yeah right. Filling in forms. It is up there on my CV along with making tea and cleaning up body fluids.

I talked about just saying no in tip 52, but sometimes we need to be a little more ingenious in making sure we aren't roped into tasks that aren't what we are supposed to be doing. For example, I have been known to explain that I haven't got as much knowledge as so-and-so about the child concerned, so if I came into the process now, it would mean duplicating information and giving other people more work to do as they got me up to speed, and there-fore slowing down the whole process. And we wouldn't want that, would we?

As SENDCOs, we need to be crystal clear that our role lies alongside that of the class teacher. I have found myself in situations where, inadvertently, my 'I'm just trying to be helpful' intervention has been counterproductive. In speaking on behalf of the teacher, I said what the teacher wouldn't have said, and ended up giving us both more hassle than either of us needed.

I think we underestimate how accepting others will be when we say no, especially when we say it in a positive, firm and kind manner.

92. GETTING TO KNOW YOU

When I rule the world – and it is just a question of time – I will ban anyone from going up to a SENDCO and uttering the line, 'I've got one for you …' especially when it is delivered at the beginning of the academic year when new children have just joined the school. I have heard this said so many times in my career, and my response is always the same: 'How much have you liaised with the previous class teacher? How much time have you taken to get to know the child before coming to darken my door while my cuppa goes cold?'

I can take this hard line from experience. When I was a class teacher, with three year groups in my class, I always spent the first half-term getting to know the new children and taking them under my wing. This paved the way for building great connections with the children new to my class. In this way, come the first half-term holiday of the year, I could talk about the individual children – their likes and dislikes, needs and abilities – in such a way that they really felt valued.

The first half-term or so is an important time to get to know the parents too. We need to ensure that we communicate with them as much as possible about their children, and make it obvious how much we care about their children as individuals. The time invested in these children and their families will repay itself many times over, and the sooner you make that investment in getting to know the child, the sooner the pay-off. It is so much more rewarding than, 'I've got another one for you, Mrs Bootman.'

93. YOU CAN'T BEAT A GOOD PUPIL PROGRESS MEETING

As a SENDCO across four schools, you might think that attending pupil progress meetings would start becoming a tad tedious. You couldn't be further from the truth. To be at such meetings, alongside caring and committed school leaders and classroom teachers, is a genuine privilege.

What makes for a great pupil progress meeting is the quality of the dialogue, and it is so refreshing and inspiring to bring my SENDCO voice and perspective to these conversations. It is through these meetings that I get to know about the children in our schools, the support they are receiving and the further support they require. This is joined-up thinking in action – a great example of the patchwork quilt of care we discussed in tip 90.

I make notes at each meeting, which I can then refer back to during the year as I start to piece together an accurate overview of what is happening – and what needs to happen – in each class and in school. In this way, I can also start to spot trends, overlaps and gaps, allowing me to target any internal or external training in a precise and effective way. And I get a cuppa at each meeting. What's not to like?

94. THE IMPORTANCE OF THE FULL STORY

One of the biggest lessons I have learned in my role as a SENDCO is to always find out the full story. Regardless of whether I am talking to children, staff or parents, it is important that everyone feels they can tell their story in full and in their own words.

When we ensure this happens, it means we are actively listening and assimilating what the other person has got to say. In the busy world in which we live, it is all too easy to jump to conclusions, seek short cuts or pounce on a quick way to solve a problem. But we don't know what went on at home that morning or what is waiting at home that evening. We don't know what happened over the week-end or what is going on in the wider family unit.

Only when we give individuals the time to explain how they feel can we truly unpick what is happening, helping them to feel genuinely valued and listened to in the pro-cess. Isn't that what all of us want?

For the particular children in our care, it doesn't have to be the big things that cause the deepest upset. A missed breakfast, the wrong jumper, itchy socks, a lost shoe, an unusual item in a packed lunch – these seemingly insig-nificant events can cause huge distress for children even before they come through the school gates. By providing an open and safe environment, where everyone can safely explain how they are feeling, we can ensure that we are doing our bit to get the day back on track.

It isn't just the children whose day might have got off to a bad start. Perhaps a member of staff comes into school and seems terse and standoffish with you. Only later do you find out that they received some bad news on the way to work. Ah, that explains it, and you continue down the empathy road, from which you may have inadvertently strayed if you had presumed rather than paused. The empathy road has a speed limit, so remember to stick to it.

Get the full story, let people talk, don't jump to conclusions and take a breath before you respond. In this way, wonderful professional relationships are built and sustained.

95. CHECK IN, NOT UP

As SENDCOs, our time is precious. We know the 101 things we have got to do before midday and, as a result, we might not have time to ensure that our emails and messages don't come across as overly officious. Then we wonder why we have put the back up of whoever was on the receiving end of that terse one-liner, making them wary and anxious that we are about to catch them out.

One way to address this issue is to think about your communication with parents and colleagues as *checking in with them* rather than *checking up on them*. This subtle change can make all the difference, believe me.

When I was an inexperienced teacher and was told that random exercise books were going to be taken in for a book scrutiny, I would take all my books home and over-mark them, so I couldn't be accused of not doing my job properly. The findings of everyone's book scrutiny were circulated to the whole staff – *pour encourager les autres*, I presume – with negative comments in red and positive ones in green. As you might imagine, such an inhumane system had the opposite effect to the one it was seeking. We hadn't been told what would be looked at in the process, the method of feedback was cruel and demoralising, and there was no direct conversation between the scrutiniser and the scrutinised.

As awful as that experience was, it taught me a lot. Now, I ensure that all of my colleagues are aware of my expectations, and I do my best to give sensible timescales for completing them. I assume that everyone is doing their best, so they don't need me to check up on them but to check in with them to see how things are going and whether they need any more support (or time). Sometimes, it might be that what I need them to do hasn't worked its way to the top of their extensive and ever-changing to-do list and a little positive nudge from me bumps it up a few places.

Checking in is a two-way process. I had a colleague who hadn't filled in the paperwork I needed from her for an EHCP. She then emailed me to say she felt overwhelmed by it all and could I meet her to go through it. In other words, she was checking in with me. Great. We met and went through the first part of the paperwork, after which she said, 'This isn't as difficult as I thought. I'll take it from here, thank you.' Much better than a terse 'get a move on' email, don't you think?

96. SPECIAL SCHOOLS REALLY ARE SPECIAL

I recently had the pleasure of working directly with our local special school, and what an amazing experience it was. What blew me away was how happy and animated the children were and yet how calm the setting. The children in this school were thriving because the professionals around them believed in them and valued them 100%.

I would recommend that all SENDCOS approach their local special school to go and look round, just to see how it works on a day-to-day basis. This is not to duplicate what special schools do in your own setting but to open your mind to how others are supporting children with additional and complex needs.

For example, one thing I came away with from my visit was the importance of the children spending time outside. I started looking for ways I could make the outdoors an extension of our classrooms to benefit all children but especially our children with additional needs. From this visit, I was able to help make the learning a far more rich, multisensory and healthy experience.

97. SEE THE WORLD THROUGH THE EYES OF THE CLASS TEACHER

We all have our jobs to do, but the class teacher has their job to do and then some. Seeing the world through their eyes is an important aspect of the SENDCO's work, and one that can make or break positive working relationships.

For SENDCOs to be effective in supporting our class teachers, it is vital that they trust us, particularly if we are to have 'buy-in' for the suggestions we put forward. Transparency is critical, as is understanding their limitations and fully acknowledging their personal and professional perspective.

We have all been in a meeting when an outside agent has told us which interventions need to be put in place. We all nod, but before their car has even left the school car park, we are already muttering about how unrealistic the suggestions are and how it will never work. We carry on as before, but with a growing sense of foreboding as we know they will be back soon to ask us how we are getting on.

In such circumstances, the SENDCO can be a wonderful ally to the busy teacher by voicing doubts about lack of time or resources or inadequate training to make the suggestion work. We need to be human and keep things human for everyone else. When a class teacher says they can't deliver an intervention, try to see it through their eyes. Acknowledge what they are saying and why they are saying it. Recognise that they want the best for the child but that this suggestion isn't workable, at least not in its current guise.

With this empathetic approach, you can then work with them to look at how to overcome this obstacle, and do it together. Perhaps you need to unpick it first? Perhaps it needs to be broken down into smaller chunks? Perhaps it would be useful for you to model it in the classroom initially? Perhaps a team-teaching approach would provide the best start?

The worst thing that can happen is for you to blithely toss a suggestion to a teacher without any thought for their working life, and for them to feel they have failed by not making it work, and letting down the child and the school in the process. As a SENDCO, make sure you are part of a supportive network, so teachers feel able to be honest about what they think they can and can't provide in their classrooms.

98. I LIKE YOUR COAT!

Making someone feel noticed and appreciated costs nothing, but it can transform their day. I was speaking at an event in a town I hadn't visited before, so I was feeling a little anxious as I stepped off the train at the station. Suddenly, a complete stranger came up to me and said, 'I like your coat.' What an instant way to put a spring in my step. Wow!

Why don't we do this more in our schools, with the children, their parents and our colleagues? 'I love what you've done with your hair.' 'I really like your shoes.' 'I'm loving your new bag/pencil case/flask/brother.' 'That coat is just fab.' It doesn't have to be much, but it shows you notice and value the person to whom you are speaking. And who, young or old, doesn't want a bit of that on a grey Thursday in November?

What you are doing here is consciously and authentically building connections with those around you, which will pay off both in the short and long term, as well as making someone feel positive about themselves. In many ways, what you compliment is less important than the fact that you do. When we make personal connections, especially with children, they begin to feel safe and valued. Furthermore, the connections turn into other connections, like a kindness ripple spreading out across the school – and all because someone liked your coat.

99. MIRROR MIRROR

We mirror what we see on a daily basis. Think back to your childhood and the experiences you had then – the things you saw and heard growing up from parents, grandparents and peers – that have moulded you into the adult you are today. Day by day, children become what they see around them.

To me, this is as fascinating as it is scary as it is empowering. Through our every action, we are a mirror for the children in our care from which they will learn to copy. It is important, therefore, that we are conscious of this and display the values and beliefs we want them to embed now and in the future.

This mirroring isn't just for the children. Parents and colleagues also learn to copy us, so we need to be mindful of what it is they see. As before, taking a breath and pausing before we speak or act means we can assess what we are going to do next and ensure it provides the best possible reflection for all concerned.

100. BEING A SENDCO IN MORE THAN ONE SCHOOL

In the old days, life for SENDCOs was fairly straightforward, if a little predictable. You worked in a school, no ruffices were required and your car was how you got to work, not where you did your work. Now, many of us have been swept up by a MAT and you might find yourself, like me, working across multiple schools which just happen to have the same head office.

If you are offered this opportunity, then I would recommend that you take it. If you are considering being a SENDCO across several schools, it is important that you don't see it as two or more times the work you have to do presently, as much of what you do in one school can be transposed to the others.

That said, it is inescapable that you are spreading yourself between schools in the MAT. When I first began in my current role, I had two Ofsted inspections in quick succession – one in the 'mother school', where I had been working for sixteen years or so, and the other in a new school. I was able to take systems that I had developed successfully in the original school and, with a bit of tweaking, make them work in the new school. As a result, both inspections went smoothly.

If you do find yourself working as a SENDCO in more than one school, my top tip is to make yourself as visible as possible in the first term. As the late Queen Elizabeth II used to say, 'We have to be seen to be believed.' Get to know the staff and let them get to know you. I also made sure that the parents in my new schools knew who I was too. They knew my name and could pick me out in a police line-up if necessary. I also aim to have lots of meetings – face to face, virtually and even old school with a phone to my ear – to ensure I am beginning to connect with them.

I go into the staffroom and talk to staff as much as possible, even if I am just passing through. I also try to spend time around the children, for my sake as much as theirs. This often happens as what I call a 'yum-yum'. A yum-yum is what you do when, for example, you are knee-deep in paperwork and need a break to breathe and regroup. This is the point when I go walkabout and meet live, unpredictable, fabulous children. I often wander into a reception class and join in with their lesson. Not only does this ground me, but it also helps me to remember that all the paperwork I do when I am stuck in my office makes a difference to real children in our care. I spoke to a group of SENDCOs recently and one of them announced, 'I'm going to find my yum-yum time, Ginny.'

Yum-yum time can definitely reinvigorate. For example, I went for a walk recently and a child who has communication difficulties grabbed my hand and said, 'We go to music,' and so off I went to join in, unexpectedly but joyously, with a music lesson. These are the times that remind us why we do what we do. That impromptu visit led to a great chat with the class teacher about this super pupil. The more I just pop in to classes, the more teachers expect me to, so when I go in for an observation, it isn't seen as a big deal. I would much rather have, 'Oh, it's you again,' when I poke my head round the classroom door than, 'What are you doing here?' or 'Can I help you?' or 'Hello, are you lost?'

101. LITTLE MISS MEDIATOR

I have been referred to on more than one occasion as Little Miss Mediator. When I first asked why, I was told that it was because of my behaviour in meetings. Apparently, I was a dab hand at listening to all the points of view put forward, bringing them together and feeding them back, without anybody feeling judged or ignored.

Mediation achieves a number of things. When someone's ideas and thoughts are fed back to the group by a third party, it ensures the speaker knows they have been heard. This is important: even if you don't agree with someone, they need to know you are at least listening. It also makes what is being said less emotive. If we feel passionate about something, that passion can get in the way of putting our point across in a clear way. And if we are in a position of authority – or genuinely desperate – hearing the words from someone else can make them a whole lot less threatening than they perhaps first appeared.

Diplomacy is so important in meetings where various stakeholders – staff, parents, outside agencies and so on – are present. I would definitely recommend that you get some training in mediation skills if they don't come naturally to you. However, it is often in disputes and disagreements between staff members where you will earn your Little Miss Mediator badge most frequently.

There are two main aspects to the role. The first is to help your colleagues see each other's point of view – a key tenet as we travel along the empathy road. In education, we can often become institutionalised (in how many other jobs do you have to announce your intention to visit the bathroom?). The SENDCO is well placed to be professional, to help find the middle ground and to smooth the way for a solution to be found without anyone feeling they have either lost or compromised excessively. After all, a compromise involves working together to find a new solution that no one had thought of before but that we all now agree on, and that is a great result.

This is where the second aspect of your role comes into play. You are not only channelling the ideas and positions coming from various sides of the table (and joining the dots between them), but you are also ideally placed to add some ideas of your own – ideas that it takes a SENDCO to see. Your secret weapon is to bring other people's ideas together along with insights of your own to produce that previously unidentified solution. It might not happen every time, but 'seek, and ye shall find'. If you believe a better answer is out there somewhere, for the most part you will find it.

One of the main times this mediation role is needed is around the thorny annual subject of teaching assistants' timetables. It is very much a situation where demand outstrips supply (which, if I know anything about economics, means they should be paid a fortune!). As teachers, we can become possessive about teaching assistants, and understandably so. Having another professional adult in the room is not only beneficial for our children, but it can also be the only thing that keeps us on the right side of sanity. Divvying up who gets what teaching assistant when and for how long can therefore lead to a fraught meeting. The SENDCO can be the person who is just enough removed to help everyone see why certain decisions have been made.

I sometimes think of my role as like making a casserole (comfort food analogies are among my favourites). Everyone's ingredients go into the pot, and my job is not only to stir but also to add the seasoning, so everyone agrees that it tastes just right. I am feeling hungry now.

102. HOW DO WE TEACH KINDNESS?

There is an easy answer to the question of how we teach kindness: we model it. By being kind to the children in our care, by being kind to our colleagues and, importantly, by being kind to ourselves, we are teaching why being kind is important and how to do it.

You can have the word 'kindness' as a school value on a website, laminated on a lanyard or displayed on the wall, but unless it is built into the day-to-day actions and inter-actions of all staff, you may as well as have 'time travel' as part of your school's mission statement.

Kindness isn't something you put on; it is something you exude. It lives inside us and shows itself naturally when it is needed, not forced out through gritted teeth. The next time you are walking around your school, look out for kind-ness. Are there examples of it inside and outside the building? Are all the adults modelling it? Would a visitor know that kindness was a school value without being told? And, the ultimate litmus test, do the children exhibit kindness to one another, without being pressed into it by adults? If they do, then you know you are doing something right. Well done!

Saying no (as we have seen in tips 52 and 91) is a form of kindness too. By politely declining to do something that would bring you unnecessary stress or take you away from supporting your children, you are being kind to yourself. By not beating yourself up for little mistakes, by patting yourself on the back for trying new things, regardless of the result, by taking the acclaim and by allowing yourself to feel good when things go well, you are exemplifying self-kindness. This will help the children to understand the importance of being kind to yourself.

Mirror neurons are a type of brain cell that fire when we perform an action and when we observe someone else perform that action. What is being reflected in the brains of the children by the actions of the adults in your school?

103. THE APPLE OF KINDNESS

I had been supporting the boy for nearly two years. He lived in a world where he was too busy surviving to be able to think about being kind to others. Who could blame him? If you have never known kindness, how can you show it? Yet, as a school, we knew we couldn't give up on him. That would have been unkind.

At the time, I used to have a basket of fruit in my class-room. Children who wanted some fruit could help themselves, no questions asked. The little boy came to me at the beginning of the day and said he was hungry. I told him to help himself from the fruit basket. Today's choice – tangerine or banana. He returned to my desk and informed me that he didn't like tangerines or bananas and could he please have an apple.

It would have been easy to reply, 'No, sorry, there aren't any apples. It's a tangerine or a banana or nothing – you choose,' but I didn't. I remembered I had an apple in my bag as part of my packed lunch and promptly gave it to him. I didn't make a big thing of it. I just gave an apple to a little boy who wanted an apple. He took the apple away but then, a minute or so later, he was back. He wanted me to cut the apple in half for him. Again, it would have been easy (and it was tempting) to say, 'Just eat it as it is,' but I didn't. I found a knife, cut it in two and handed it back to him. He stood there, looking at the apple and then, holding out one piece, said, 'You must have half the apple. It was your apple, so we must have half each.'

Oh, my goodness, that story gets me every time. It shows the impact that a kindness-based approach can have on the children in our care. Next time when you don't think you have a minute to talk to that child, please remember the apple of kindness and act accordingly. Not quite *James and the Giant Peach*, but not far off.

Do you remember when certain items in supermarkets were limited during lockdown? At one point, pasta, toilet rolls and, yes, you guessed it … peaches were on the list. I happened to be in a queue for the tills one day when I heard the cashier tell the woman in front of me that she wasn't able to buy all three tins of peaches, as only two were allowed. The shopper explained that they were for her elderly father who loved peaches; however, the cashier was adamant that the rules were the rules. At this point, I interjected and said that I would buy the extra tin of peaches for the woman. She was so thankful, and I duly bought them and gave them to her, thinking no more of it.

A few minutes later, as I fought with my trolley, it and I having different ideas as to where we should be going, I heard a female voice calling out. I looked up and saw the tin of peaches lady beckoning me towards her, so I wandered over. As I got closer, I could see that she was on her mobile, and she announced excitedly that she had her father on the phone. She had told him about my kindness and he wanted to thank me in person. And so ensued a lovely chat with the gentleman about his love for peaches and how I had 'made his day'. My point is that all I did was buy a tin of peaches, but that small act of kindness made such a difference to an individual.

104. BUILDING TRUST TAKES TIME; LOSING TRUST TAKES SECONDS

Fundamentally, most SENDCOs are bridge builders, not bridge burners. A bridge, by definition, allows two sides to come together on one side or the other or even in the middle. However, building a bridge is a painstaking, slow and potentially risky project.

The task of building bridges often falls to the SENDCO. I am more than happy to build bridges because I know the care I will take to make them solid and long lasting. Bridge builders need to be able to put their ego to one side and forgo notions of hierarchy. Putting the child at the centre of everything we do means we are all in it together, and giving and taking is easier when we all want the same thing.

I remember an occasion when a parent and I disagreed about the best course of action for their child. I could have dug my heels in as the professional expert, but I stopped, took a breath, thought about what had been said, and then agreed to the course of action the parent was proposing. I trusted them and they needed to see that I trusted them. This wasn't about me losing face but accepting that the parent knew their child best. It was also another brick in the bridge of trust we were building – something that paid off many times over.

105. LISTEN TO THE QUIET VOICES

Time is precious. We can march through a meeting at breakneck speed and inadvertently hear only the loud voices, believing they are the voices of the whole group. There is another side, though, and those of us who make our educational pilgrimage along the empathy road need to take heed of it.

No matter what sort of meeting you are in – with staff, parents or even other family members – make sure you are listening hard to the people who are saying nothing. So often, in my experience, the quiet ones are thinking and reflecting, percolating if you like, the most. If you assume their quietness indicates a lack of understanding or interest, then you may well miss an opportunity to hear an important voice. They might only have one thing to say, but, goodness, how important it can be.

The quiet voices will remain quiet unless we ask them to speak up, so make a point of inviting these individuals to meetings and asking for their thoughts and reflections. Open questions are far more useful in encouraging people to speak than closed questions: 'Is there anything you would like to be clarified?' 'Is there anything you think I have forgotten?'

This applies to the online world too. I took part in a Zoom meeting during lockdown and a number of the individuals involved were very vocal in making their views heard. However, one of the little boxes on my screen contained the face of someone who was clearly just sitting and thinking about what was going on, even though they hadn't said a word. Part way through the meeting, I invited them to speak and, with everyone else on mute, including me, they gave a remarkably balanced and considered over-view of the situation, including a suggestion about what we might do, which went on to change the way we worked with the child in question.

106. A QUICK WORD ON BEING ENDLESSLY FASCINATED

I am regularly fascinated by what is going on around me. It is a state that goes beyond mere curiosity. I genuinely marvel at what people do, how they react and what happens next. I am convinced that this approach helps to keep my stress levels down (mostly). Rather than cursing others or kicking myself, or vice versa, I simply look at what is happening and revel in it. How interesting that she thinks that. How curious that he said that. How abso-flipping-lutely fascinating that this happened.

It also means that you are constantly learning. Rather than judging, pigeonholing or throwing your hands up in despair, defeat or despondency, you are always looking for the reasons why something happened, so you can create a better outcome next time. People are endlessly fascinat-ing, and as SENDCOs we get to work with some of the most interesting people on the planet. So, look with fresh eyes and enjoy what each remarkable day throws at you.

107. CHANGE YOUR MIND; PROVE YOU HAVE GOT ONE

Changing your mind is a sign of strength, not weakness. As I mentioned in tip 95, when I first came into teaching I would double-mark my books at the merest whiff of an impending book scrutiny. If there was a lesson observation coming up, I would be in my classroom until late redoing the displays (yes, including the borders). Looking back, what drove me wasn't simply the desire to do my best for the children in my care, although I clearly did want that. It was also the fear of being found out, of not being good enough, of being an imposter. I know I am not alone in this.

Now – whether through age, experience, confidence or a combination of all three – my thinking has changed, and I feel so much better for it. I still want to do my best for the children, but these days my best is good enough. This isn't about arrogance or having a closed mindset. I am always humble enough to learn and happy enough to change. It is about accepting that none of us can do more than our best, so our best will have to do.

As SENDCOs, we are all passionate about what we do, and most of us perform to the best of our ability. We can't know everything, though, and acknowledging this shows our human side. Again, it is a strength, not a weakness. If you need to change tack part-way through, that is okay. This lady is for turning!

For example, I was leading a meeting recently which, in my head at least, was about simply passing on information to my teaching colleagues about a new form I needed them to complete. What could possibly go wrong? The quick chat turned into a heavy discussion about their concerns, and I realised that my new-fangled form wasn't going to help matters. Listening to the expertise of the teachers, I changed my mind mid-meeting and we went off in a different and better direction, with everyone happy, including me.

108. ARE WE MAKING OUR CHILDREN INDEPENDENT OR DEPENDENT?

There might just be two letters separating 'independent' from 'dependent' but those two letters can change everything for a child. It is vital, whether we are a SENDCO, class teacher or any other adult in the life of a child, that we never lose sight of independence as one of our key goals.

If the parent is constantly speaking for their child, they will not only not speak for themselves, but they will never learn how to do it. If the teacher is constantly doing things for the child, even for all the right reasons, they will never learn to do things for themselves. I have seen children becoming so reliant on a teaching assistant that they flounder when expected to work independently. It is essential to have whatever support is needed in the classroom, but also to ensure that the systems in place demand and expect periods of independent work.

For example, giving a child a task that is just below the level at which they are working at helps to build their confidence. They can then they go on to trickier tasks but from a starting point of success, not failure. Having a sense that they will be able to use what they are learning one day the next day helps here too; it can be overwhelming if every lesson is always about learning new things. Spaced retrieval practice that deepens understanding and reinforces knowledge is so important. Knowing you will be using what you have learned independently sets up an expectation of purpose and achievement, which is great for motivation and engagement in all of us, young and old.

It is like learning a new language. Personally, I want to be given vocabulary that I can use over and over again, with picture cues to help me. By adding to this daily using a simple and well-thought-through system, I would feel confident in what I was doing. If I was given new words every day, but without picture cues, I would feel lost. I use this analogy often with colleagues to show how best to help children gain independence. We all like structure, and we all like to understand what is being asked of us.

109. WHEN THE REFERRAL MAZE MEETS THE POSTCODE LOTTERY

One of the first things to do when making a referral is to find out which address to use. This will ensure that you at are at least knocking on the right door from the start. I work across four schools, which are located across three different postcodes, so I have found this out the hard way.

Referrals may rely on the home postcode or the school postcode. I have also known them to be based on the postcode of the child's GP. It wouldn't be unusual for a child to live in one county, go to school in another and have a doctor in a third. For this reason, check, check and check again which address you need to use for the referral and which local authority needs to be involved.

NHS referrals often employ the GP's address for determining the relevant authority, whereas school-based services are more likely to use the school's address. That said, these can also revert back to the home address. I told you it was a maze. I have a chart on my wall to identify the different pathways that might be involved – something I can't recommend highly enough. If you are playing the lottery, at least make sure you have the right numbers.

110. LITTLE MISS TRANSLATOR

My other nomenclature of choice is Little Miss Translator. As SENDCOs, we are often called on to make sense of and translate what is happening, whether for the teacher, the parents or even the child.

For example, when a report is received from an outside agency, it often falls to us to act as an interface between the agency, the parents and the staff. We are the ones with the key to unlocking the report. We are able to help make sure the teacher isn't overwhelmed and understands clearly what is being asked of them. We can also help the parents to understand what is happening, the thinking behind the decision and what will – or perhaps won't – happen next.

Our unique position, experience and knowledge means we can act as an educational voice of reason. We often view things through various lenses, so we can help others to see different perspectives and points of view in a way that isn't emotionally charged.

What is more, with class teachers so busy juggling all the many educational balls they have in the air at any one time, we can also act as a filter. We are best placed to sift out the information they need from the information they don't have to bother with. You are the bit in the coffee machine that hangs on to the leftover coffee grounds while the teacher enjoys a great espresso. You are the strainer making sure they get tea without leaves. You are the sieve so they just get the nuggets of gold.

Of course, sometimes you are both the class teacher and the SENDCO. I have been in that fortunate position (and have been head at the same time), so you might end up talking to yourself quite a bit, but you will save time and shouldn't have too many arguments.

111. PUTTING THE 'FUN' INTO FUNDING

It might not sound like a great date, but if you are ever invited to your local high needs funding (LHNF) panel meeting, do say yes. I had the chance to attend a couple of years ago, and it gave me a different insight into the whole process.

The LHNF panel was made up of individuals from various aspects of education, who had all spent many hours beforehand looking through the applications and analysing them in detail. The time and care spent prior to the meeting was impressive in and of itself. It was a very human process.

At the top of the agenda was a discussion around the specific and best ways to help the children move forward with their learning, with the aim of putting in support for them as early as possible. The reason for this was that they wanted the children to become as independent as they could as soon as they could and, wherever possible, to stay within a mainstream setting.

It struck me that while this was a panel of caring professionals, they weren't mind readers. I realised that it is down to us as SENDCOs to give them as full a picture as we can of each child and their unique situation. When LHNF panels have the bigger picture, they stand a much better chance of seeing what the needs are and making the right call.

Seeing how my own applications were discussed helped me to reconsider how I approached my end of the application process. One thing I did as a result was to enlist the support of a SEND consultant who was a bit of a whiz when it came to filling in referral forms. I invited her to explain the process to me and the other SENDCOs in the MAT. She was able to unpick the process and break it down into bite-size chunks. We were also able to ask her questions that might not have been appropriate in a larger group.

One of the 'Well, duh!' moments during this training was realising that if we don't add something to the application, the panel won't know about it, so if in doubt, add it to the application. Feel free to quote reports and give any data-driven evidence that is robust enough to stand up to scrutiny by the panel – for example, percentiles and standardised scores in educational psychologist reports. Our funding application processes are now much stronger – not 100%, but whose are?! And all as a result of saying yes to attending that LHNF meeting.

112. THERE ISN'T JUST ONE PATHWAY TO TREAD

The days are gone of the educational psychologist being the only person with all the answers. Wonderful though they undoubtedly are, there are more of us SENDCOs than there are of them, and time and money are tighter than ever. What this means is that we have to know how to find the help and support we need without waiting for the educational psychologist to walk through the door with a golden elixir that will answer all our questions and prayers.

It is helpful to compile an index of the different agencies out there. I never stop looking for outside organisations that can support my children, staff and parents, so make sure you keep it up to date too. This then acts as a reference resource for all staff. The better our understanding of the specific needs of a child, the better we can match that need with the support offered by a particular agency. We can then also get the parents on board through consistent transparency, dialogue and reassurance.

113. HOW TO MAKE AN OUTSIDE AGENT YOUR FRIEND

Everyone is busy and, as it is in any professional setting, time is money. However, if there is one benefit from what we all went through during the pandemic, it is that we all know our way round a virtual meeting, so make the most of this new-found skill. I have celebrated online meetings in tips 25 and 26 for the flexibility they bring to our dealings with colleagues and parents, but they are useful in our interactions with outside agencies too.

At the end of a face-to-face multi-agency meeting recently, I suggested that people could join remotely for our next one, if that was what they preferred. Everyone responded so positively, with those who had travelled the furthest to get there the most ecstatic, that I had never been so popular among my peers.

FINAL THOUGHTS

My journey began over thirty years ago, with my training in Liverpool and my first 'proper' job in Gateshead. Looking back (gosh, I sound ancient don't I?), I now realise that even in those early days, I had an affinity for the amazing children who needed professional adults in their lives who wanted to take the time to understand them. By changing and tweaking a worksheet here, by listening to parents there, without being aware of it at the time, the seeds of my SENDCO-dom were being sown.

It is the little things that make the difference to the children in our care, whether it is a conversation with teachers, children or parents, allowing a child to eat their lunch in a particular order or seated in a place that suits their needs, or little thoughtful acts, like the apple of kindness boy (not to mention the tin of peaches woman), these seemingly trivial acts are what can make a big difference.

As SENDCOs, we can help children, often against the odds. When the system seems to be working against us, we can give them what they need in the here and now. I know we never have enough time, but I hope that the many time-saving tips in this book will free up time to do what I refer to as the yum-yums – those precious moments we get to spend with the wonderful children in our care. We help to provide a spider's web of trust for these children, and my hope is that this book will have helped you to consider which threads are already strong and which need strengthening further.

I also hope that you will see how having a curious and open mindset as you go about your work means you are always open to ideas and improvements, wherever they may be hiding. In this way, we are all continually striving to be even better at the important work we do transforming the lives and opportunities of the children who are counting on us the most.

We are all constantly learning. We are all on a learning journey following our own individual path. Once we understand that we don't need to be in charge all the time, or be right all the time, then that journey becomes far more wide-reaching. Can you think of a time when you have put up a barrier to something someone has suggested, and then wondered what might have happened if you had been more open and gone with it? Well, why not give it a try next time?

We are the result of the path we have chosen to follow – it makes us what we are. We now need to consider the road we are going to take next. I always refer back to Robert Frost's poem 'The Road Not Taken', which I studied at A level and still resonates with me.[1] We need to consider travelling on the less trodden path in order to make the most difference to the children in our care.

---

1   See https://www.poetryfoundation.org/poems/44272/the-road-not-taken.

978-178135337-0

978-178135338-7

978-178135339-4

978-178135340-0

978-178135341-7

978-178135369-1

978-178135373-8

978-178135400-1

978-178135353-0

ındependent thinking press ✗

www.independentthinkingpress.com

INDEPENDENT THINKING ON RESTORATIVE PRACTICE

BUILDING RELATIONSHIPS, IMPROVING BEHAVIOUR AND CREATING STRONGER COMMUNITIES

978-178135338-7

MARK FINNIS

A practical and inspiring introduction to the use of restorative practice in schools in order to improve behaviour, foster a more caring culture and forge relationships that work.

For those educators who are uncomfortable with the punitive world of zero tolerance, isolation booths and school exclusions, Mark Finnis – one of the UK's leading restorative practice experts – is here to show you that there is another way.

Drawing on his many years' experience of working with schools, social services and local government across the country, Mark shares all you need to know about what restorative practice is, how it works, where to start and the many benefits of embedding it in any educational organisation that genuinely has people at its heart.

From coaching circles and the power of doing things 'with' (and not 'to') children and young people, to moving your values off lanyards and posters and into the lived experience of every member of the school community, readers will discover how restorative practice – when done well – can transform every aspect of school life.

INDEPENDENT THINKING ON TEACHING AND LEARNING

DEVELOPING INDEPENDENCE AND RESILIENCE IN ALL TEACHERS AND LEARNERS

JACKIE BEERE

978-178135339-4

Jackie Beere's *Independent Thinking on Teaching and Learning* is a practical guide full of educational wisdom to help teachers make a genuine difference to the lives of every young person in their classroom.

All the evidence shows that the most valuable asset in any classroom is the teacher at the front. No matter what changes are made to systems or to the curriculum, one certainty remains: children will be helped or hindered in their learning, job prospects, life chances and, indeed, happiness by the teachers they come across during their time in the education system.

In this all-encompassing book on teaching and learning, Independent Thinking Associate Jackie Beere draws on her many years' experience as a teaching assistant, primary teacher and secondary head teacher to re-energise every teacher's passion for their profession.

She champions both children and teachers as learners, and – together with expert advice on how to instil the habits of independent learning in all pupils – shares great practice that delivers outstanding outcomes for all educators.

Essential reading for all teachers and school leaders who wish to make an impact on the teaching and learning in their school.

INDEPENDENT THINKING ON TRANSITION

FOSTERING BETTER COLLABORATION BETWEEN PRIMARY AND SECONDARY SCHOOLS

DAVE HARRIS

978-178135340-0

When it comes to looking at the quality of our current schooling system, the biggest elephant in the room is transition. We do it the way we've always done it and, in so many ways and despite our best intentions, we often end up doing it badly.

But, as ever, there is another way.

Which is where Independent Thinking Associate Dave Harris comes in. With an impressive track record in leadership that includes establishing one of England's all-too-rare all-through 3–18 state schools, Dave knows first-hand how much can be achieved when all phases work together and keep the children, not the system, at the heart of all they do.

In this book he tackles school transition head-on, sharing a wealth of practical approaches and vividly illustrating how primary and secondary schools can better collaborate to ensure their pupils enjoy a smooth and effective move between the two phases.

Dave's passion for joined-up thinking between different phases shines through in his writing, as does his ingenuity when it comes to the design and delivery of programmes that work. He provides a clear explanation of the differences between transition and induction programmes, and also shares a comprehensive set of appendices in which he presents a range of materials to support the ideas put forward in the book.

Suitable for all school leaders – from heads of department and heads of year to head teachers and transition leads – in primary and secondary schools.

INDEPENDENT THINKING ON EMOTIONAL LITERACY

A PASSPORT TO INCREASED CONFIDENCE, ENGAGEMENT AND LEARNING

RICHARD EVANS

978-178135373-8

Independent Thinking on Emotional Literacy shares an approach that will help educators boost their pupils' emotional literacy, with the broader aim of nurturing a more grounded, engaged and intrinsically motivated child.

Do teachers truly understand their pupils? And do the pupils themselves really understand their own needs?

In *Independent Thinking on Emotional Literacy*, Richard Evans reminds every school educator that behind every child is a set of circumstances so entwined – and within them a set of emotions so involved – that to ignore them is to be complicit in any educational failings.

Richard's aim in this book is to help improve and harness both the educator's and their pupils' emotional literacy by promoting discussion around the often-unspoken issues that prevent children from making progress at school. He also shares with teachers a tailor-made passport template to start them on the road to deeper pupil understanding – whether it's for the girl who falls asleep at the back, the boy who needs constant support on a daily basis, or those pupils who'll need extra careful attention at parents' evening.

independent thinking

Independent Thinking. An education company.

Taking people's brains for a walk since 1994.

We use our words.

www.independentthinking.com